MATT KENSETH

||||| NASCAR®

ABOVE AND BEYOND

(photo by Action Sports Photography Inc./Walter Arce)

Coordinating Editor:
Lynnette A. Bogard

Interior Design, Project Manager, Photo Imaging & Dust Jacket Design:
Christine Mohrbacher

Publisher:
Peter Bannon

Senior Managing Editors:
Joseph J. Bannon, Jr. and Susan Moyer

Copy Editor:
Holly Birch

NASCAR is a registered trademark of the National Association for Stock Car Auto Racing, Inc.

www.sportspublishingllc.com

MATT KENSETH

TABLE of CONTENTS

FOREWORD
By Roy Kenseth

The last race of the 1984 season was over. My son Matt and I were on our way home. On a whim, I pulled over to the side of the road. I made a deal with Matt. We will buy a racecar and I will drive it. We will work side by side on it and learn together.

Four years later at age 16, my son got behind the wheel. As they say, the rest is history.

Many things have changed for our family since Matt has found success in the Winston Cup Series—but our family itself hasn't changed at all. Matt calls me every day. Though we mostly talk about racing, we never get out of touch about what's going on in the non-NASCAR side of our lives.

Even though Matt and his wife Katie call North Carolina home, we all look forward to the time when they come back to Cambridge for a visit. Those days are spent working and playing outside, eating together and talking.

Ask anyone and they'll tell you I'm proud of my son. I'm not surprised at his success, because I think he's the best racer out there. And it's okay to say that because I'm his dad.

I hope you enjoy this book written by my daughter Kelley. Some might think she is overshadowed by her brother's NASCAR stardom, but she remains his biggest fan.

July 2003

Roy Kenseth

Cambridge, Wisconsin

ACKNOWLEDGMENTS

This project is dedicated to and would not have been possible without the help of many of my favorite men. Thanks be to God, without Him anything I do would be useless. Thanks to my dad, Roy Kenseth, for always being interested in the things I do. Thanks to my brother, Matt Kenseth, for taking time to see what's going on in my life and always making me feel welcome in his. Thanks to my husband, Mike, who reminded me that he was going to be a rock star and I was going to be a writer...one of us better follow up on that.

Some of the text in this book was inspired by other writers who followed Matt's career. Thanks Amy Walsh and Robyn from Adair Promotions, who kept the best darn race records that I referred back to often. Thanks also to Jeff Cheatham at Roush Racing, who had quite a busy year as Matt's PR man. Thanks to Dave Drews, Rappy, and Grandma and Grandpa Kenseth for their photo contributions. A special thanks to Doug Hornickel, who has managed to capture Matt on film in a way unlike most other photographers have.

The best part of writing this book was remembering. It was a journey down memory lane about growing up in a small town with my parents and brother. The memories become more valuable as I grow older and watch my children mirror my own life. My hope for you is that you feel at home looking at a story of someone that we both care about and adding part of our story to your life.

Kelley Maruszewski

MATT KENSETH

INTRODUCTION

Matt Kenseth spent the majority of this year scoring top tens and leading the NASCAR Winston Cup point standings. The first week in November, he sealed the deal. He will go down in history as the "last NASCAR Winston Cup Champion." His presence in NASCAR Winston Cup is no longer underrated. Right now, Matt Kenseth is at the top of his game.

So why have we heard so little about him? He's not your typical southern boy, in fact, he's a Yankee. He doesn't have any family in professional racing. The press portrays Matt as an introvert, bordering on boring. They couldn't be further from the truth. Beneath his modest demeanor and boy-next-door good looks lies a complex, introspective individual with laser-like focus and subtle wit. And more importantly, he's definitely earned the respect of his fellow drivers and legions of fans. He's found a home with Jack Roush, owner of five NASCAR Winston Cup Teams and decades of experience.

Matt did not sit on the couch as a toddler dreaming he could be Dale Earnhardt. Instead, he followed his natural abilities and found he was quite interested in motors, cars, and eventually racecars. As he became aware of his local success, he dared to dream of the beginning ranks in semi-professional racing. But not until Matt was 18 did his father start to think that Matt had a chance to make it all the way to NASCAR Winston Cup racing. Little by little the offers came and the benefits followed. Today all expectations have been fulfilled and succeeded. Matt Kenseth has gone "Above and Beyond."

CHAPTER 1

BORN and RAISED

> ## " Matt was a busy and happy little boy who loved going to preschool and Sunday School. "
>
> *—Matt's mother Nicki*

O n a driver bio, it may state that Matt was born in Madison, Wisconsin, but it's only because Cambridge didn't have a hospital. The sleepy Midwest town boasted fewer than 1,000 residents in 1972 when Matt moved in, and hasn't changed much since. Born to Roy and Nicki Kenseth, Matt joined his sister Kelley in the family's home. Matt's dad was a budding entrepreneur, upholstering furniture in the family garage in the

Matt and Grandpa Helmer in 1972. *(Kenseth family photo)*

keeping the house, cooking, and being active in Bible study and neighborhood activities. His mom recalls him as "a busy and happy little boy who loved going to preschool and Sunday School."

Growing up in the rural landscape of the Midwest held much fascination for young Kenseth. His neighborhood was filled with other boys and girls his age, wide, quiet streets and large, grassy lawns. One block away, his grandparents lived in the same house on Koshkonong Creek for 57 years. Salamanders and painted turtles, muddy pants and boots, the creek was a natural draw for children. His grandfather Helmer (and grandmother Edith) worked at Melster Candy Company for 40 years until he retired at age 73. It was in back of this factory where Matt and his friends found barrels for the taking. They would spend hours constructing rafts with the barrels and scrap wood and—sink or float—they had their chance on the creek.

Matt attended the local public school where he was a good student. It was hard to concentrate on school with so many adventures waiting. Matt

evening after working full time at Schweigers, a Jefferson, Wisconsin company that made furniture. A few years later, he opened Roy's Quality Upholstery in a little shop downtown. Matt spent evenings riding with his dad to do in-home estimates or picking up and delivering furniture in the family's delivery truck. On weekends, he might catch a ride on his dad's motorcycle or Corvette. Matt's mom stayed at home, spending her time

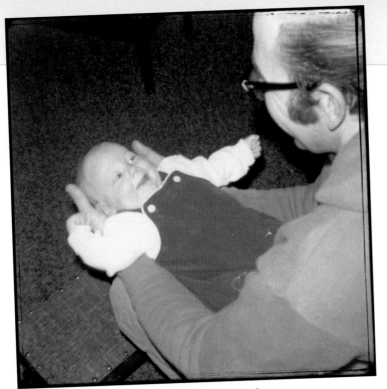

(Kenseth family photo)

played basketball and managed to enjoy shop class in high school. "I mostly remember hanging out with my friend Matt Fischer at noon hour. We liked shop because the teacher would send us into town to buy parts and we'd make the trip as long as possible."

On Sunday after church, he would take a ride in dad's Corvette to McDonald's for lunch, or stop on the side of the road to pick wildflowers for his mom. Before cable TV, Gameboy and the Internet, top entertainment of the day was Atari, and Matt mastered Asteroids and Missile Command.

It was not unusual to find Matt occupying his time with something that had wheels.
(Kenseth family photo)

MATT KENSETH

A hot summer day might have been spent swimming in the next-door neighbor's pool, shooting some basketball in the street, or maybe playing a game of kickball in the field across the street. He lived a few blocks away from school, the park and the Methodist church. His neighborhood was filled with children, and everyone played together.

In the summertime, Matt and his friends were always starting some kind of project. Whether it involved decorating bikes or wagons for the Memorial Day parade or constructing some sort of fort or hut with lawn chairs, clothespins and blankets, they were always outside doing something.

Other "sports" included whacking a tennis ball against the garage door. The best part was climbing up the TV antenna to get the balls off the roof. At night, the kids would play catch in the street, or flashlight tag until their parents finally made them come in. If Matt had to be inside, he built model cars, played with Legos, or raced his dad on his slot car race track.

Matt had a typical small-town upbringing which included baseball...however it wouldn't be long before Matt turned his attention to "faster" sports.
(Kenseth family photo)

Matt came from a middle class family. On Fridays his mom would give him one dollar to spend on things she wouldn't buy, like pop or chips. Friday nights were reserved for eating junk food and watching *The Dukes of Hazzard*. Then on Saturday mornings Matt would get up at 7:00 to watch *Superfriends*.

Growing up in a small town has contributed to Matt's laid-back demeanor. He acts and looks like the all-American boy next door. He did not aspire to escape the grasp of small town life. Yet his future talents would take him far from his little hometown.

" Ask anyone and they'll tell you I'm proud of my son. I'm not surprised at his success, because I think he's the best racer out there. "
— *Roy Kenseth*

May 1987, it would be almost another year before Matt would begin his driving career. *(Kenseth family photo)*

14

15

CHAPTER 2

A BOY CALLED MOTOR

Matt and his father, Roy, in July, 1986.
(photo courtesy of Helmer and Edith Kenseth)

Matt's grandfather Helmer owned a Simplicity riding lawnmower. When Matt was nine, he got the go-ahead to borrow the mower. The intention was that he would get the lawn mowed. The process usually resulted in some type of mechanical problem for Matt to figure out. They say lawns got mowed mighty fast when he was a boy. Roy recalls that one time they went to Piotrowski's

Matt in May, 1985 with that Simplicity mower of his grandpa Helmer's. *(Kenseth family photo)*

Lawn Repair, the place that sold old lawnmowers, and he bought one that Matt could ride and work on. The first thing Matt did was take off the mower deck and venture out on to the streets of Cambridge. Driving the mower down the street or sidewalk would only encourage people to smile and wave. Matt enjoyed fooling around with the small engine. First he replaced the gears to make it faster. By trial and error, and a little help from his dad, he developed a mechanical mind. When the family moved from Cambridge to the slightly smaller town of Rockdale (population 90), the rural neighborhood was exchanged for acreage and fields.

Next came a three-wheeler, a snowmobile, and a dirt bike, more lawnmowers and an occasional ride on Uncle John's homemade go-kart or mini-bike. Roy had thought about getting his son a go-kart, but they were too fast and didn't provide Matt with the mechanical challenges that the mowers did. (Racing go-karts hadn't yet become the popular transition into professional racing that it is today.) It was a familiar sight to see Matt on anything with wheels or a motor.

It was no surprise to Roy that Matt was a gear head. Even though Roy played basketball in high school, his interest was mainly in cars. Roy's first car was a 1949 Ford when he was 16. He had saved money from working as a paperboy from age 12 and then part-time in the drug store as a soda jerk. Roy remembers that he received a lot of tickets in his youth, mostly speeding tickets. "At times I would run straight pipes that were so loud that the cops would warn me and then finally issue a ticket. I'd take the pipes off for

It was a familiar sight to see Matt on anything with wheels or a motor.

a while and put them back on a few months later. I drove faster than what I should have driven," Roy admits. "But in those days, it wasn't drinking and driving. I drove fast because I liked cars." Roy then went into the Air Force in August of 1960 and was honorably discharged four years later. After he was married, Roy purchased a '67 Corvette and a '69 Yenko Camaro that he drag raced at Great Lakes Speedway in Union Grove and Byron. The cars he drag raced were streetcars— he'd drive down to the track and then right onto it. He and his brothers would go down there every once and a while for fun and occasionally were rewarded with a trophy.

Roy's father Helmer also liked motorcycles and airplanes and auto racing. When he was young,

Grandpa Helmer and his plane. *(photo courtesy of Helmer and Edith Kenseth)*

Matt's sister Kelley, his mom Nicki and Matt with their first race car outside the shop in May, 1985. *(photo by Aren Larson)*

he'd head down to State Fair Park and watch races. "There was very little racing around this area at that time," he said. Edith recalls Helmer was flying when "I was in high school. He was flying way back on the farm before we were married." Helmer says he didn't do too much flying while his kids were growing up. In the 1970s, Helmer and three of his sons pooled their resources to buy a small tail dragger airplane. The brothers all had permits to solo the plane, but the flying honors usually rested with their father. A few miles from their home on Clarence Falk's land was a small hangar and airstrip. It was a memorable day when Grandpa Helmer asked Matt if he wanted a ride. "We were going up to Dodge County and saw a train that must have been heading to Milwaukee. We swung around behind it and chased it until we passed it, then waved to the engineers," Helmer said of one of their flights. The many adventures of Matt Kenseth were just beginning.

Matt and his friend Dan in the Memorial Day Parade, Main Street, Cambridge. *(Kenseth family photo)*

ABOVE AND BEYOND

CHAPTER 3

A BUNCH of RACING UNCLES

One of Matt's favorite things to do was to go to his Uncle Gary's house and watch him and his other uncles work on their race car. He loved to watch them load the race car up to go to the track on Saturday night. There was a time in the early '80s when the Kenseth brothers took their turns running limited late model Chevys on the tracks of Jefferson Speedway and Columbus. His Uncle Butch drove a front-wheel drive Toronado.

On the back end there was usually a 'thanks mom & dad.'

MATT KENSETH

The dry humor that Matt is known for is a family trait—Wayne's duct-taped car number was K9 and Butch's number was OK. Roy became more interested in racing as his brothers drove. Matt's cousin Steve, who was five years older than Matt, began competitively racing a VW bug. The uncles were on a limited budget—racing for fun—content to be middle-of-the-pack cars. Sponsorship usually came from family members like their cousin who owned Korth Construction or Roy who owned Roy's La-Z-Boy Shop. On the back end there was usually a "thanks mom & dad." Many a race car was named Edith, after their mother. Grandma Kenseth's scrapbook is filled with old photos and newspaper articles along with her notes about her sons' racing.

Uncle Butch with "OK."
(photo courtesy of Helmer and Edith Kenseth)

Wayne, Butch, Gary and Roy Kenseth all racing against one another in 1981. *(photo courtesy of Helmer and Edith Kenseth)*

"**Grandpa told my dad and I how much fun he had in the car. He told us that 'it really gets into the corners!'**"

—*Matt Kenseth*

MATT KENSETH

There was never any heated competition between them; in fact, they even drove each other's cars sometimes. Edith recalls, "Once Wayne hit the pit wall at Jefferson very hard. He wasn't hurt, but his car was totally destroyed. The next day all the brothers and their kids came over to our house and started fixing it up for the next week."

"Racing at Jefferson was fun and there wasn't really any other racing around," Helmer said. He was most interested in being a spectator. "I got in the race car at Columbus and went a few times around the track to see what it felt like, that was it." Matt remembers that Uncle Gary wasn't too happy about Roy giving Helmer the keys to the race car. "Grandpa told my dad and I how much fun he had in the car. He told us that 'it really gets into the corners!'" Grandpa and Grandma Kenseth were their sons' biggest fans and attended most of the races. At age 12, Matt joined aunts, uncles, cousins and friends gathered together in the same place in the stands every Saturday night to watch what was quickly becoming a favorite family pastime.

Uncle Wayne's K-9 car.
(photo courtesy of Helmer and Edith Kenseth

The Kenseths were a blue-collar family. During World War II, Helmer worked for Northwest Airlines. They had a contract with the air transport command, and Helmer flew back and forth to Canada twice. Later, he worked as a mechanical supervisor, in charge of maintaining the machinery at the Melster Candy Company. Edith worked off

Matt was already beginning to show his racing talent by setting the fast time at Columbus, WI on May 12, 1989. His father shared the track with him with the second fastest time. *(photo courtesty of Helmer and Edith Kenseth)*

and on when she wasn't pregnant to help make ends meet. With seven children, the siblings were friends and caretakers of each other. Cambridge was a town where you could leave your house unlocked and your children playing outside. Matt's dad played in the same park and creek that his own children would play in 30 years later. The same small town values that were instilled in Matt as a young boy would carry him to heights he could never have imagined.

Roy's first victory at Columbus. *(photo courtesy of Helmer and Edith Kenseth)*

CHAPTER 4

AN INTRODUCTION to SHORT TRACKS

One afternoon the offer came. It was really a whim, Roy remembers. "We were driving home from the track at the end of the season, and I was thinking out loud." He turned to his son and said, "I think we ought to buy a race car, and I think I ought to drive it and you ought to work on it." Matt recalls, "It wasn't a deal really. My dad just decided he wanted to buy a car and turned around.

"The day they dropped the race car off, we didn't even have any tools," Matt said. "We went to Farm & Fleet so we could buy a jack and jack stands."

That was in September, and their first race was the following May. "Now that we had the race car, we didn't really know what to do with it. We started out by cleaning and painting it. We had help from Gary and Butch," Matt said.

All of Matt's free time went into learning about his dad's race car. Roy didn't know much about

Driver introductions before the ARTGO Dixieland 250 at WIR, August 1991. *(photo by Doug Hornickel)*

race cars either, and learned mostly from his brothers when they came over and worked on the cars. Matt remembers, "Once I used the wrong wrench and broke something, and I called Uncle Gary at work to come over and help me get it fixed before my dad came home. Not only did I want to finish the job, I didn't want my dad to know I broke it!" Roy experienced some success on the short tracks of Wisconsin, and Matt waited impatiently

for his turn. After Roy's first full season, they got one used car and also built a car. They spent a lot of time hanging out at chassis builder GTF Motorsports.

"When we were building the cars, we didn't really expect to run well or win features," Matt said of their beginning. "We just wanted to run laps and see if it was something we liked doing."

When Matt turned 16, he took over the wheel. Matt's first race car was a 1981 Chevrolet Camaro chassis with a price tag of $1,800. This car would speed Matt to his first victory at Columbus 151 Speedway in July of 1988.

In 1988, Matt won two Sportsman Features, and in 1989 he took the checkered flag six times at Columbus 151, the Dells, and Golden Sands in Plover. He had earned a reputation as a phenom, stunning competitors and fans alike with his early success. With an ambitious attitude, he told the press, "I know it's way off, but I hope to race a super late model in ASA someday."

Matt spent the previous winter building a 1989

Matt and his mom Nicki. *(Kenseth family photo)*

examining his wallet, and Matt's natural talent, it didn't take Roy long to see that there was only room for one driver in this family.

They owned two cars, a primary and a backup, with all their assets tied up in them. That summer, Matt was involved in his first major wreck, completely destroying their primary car in an eight-car pile-up at Slinger. The cost of the damages was $20,000.

In 1989, Matt was a junior in high school, and he spent his second summer clicking off as many laps as possible. Success seemed natural for the teenager. By the end of 1989, his success was no longer a surprise, it was mildly expected. Matt's signature style was already emerging. He was already beginning to show patience in coming through the field, restraint under pressure and always managed to save something for the last few laps. Matt's casual demeanor and youthful ambition made him a likeable addition to the Midwest circuit.

Buick Regal limited late model, outfitting it with a competitive motor, and securing a few sponsor decals. For a time, Roy thought Kenseth Racing could support a father/son race team, but that idea quickly fizzled out due to a lack of funds and sponsorship. Although stock car racing was a short-lived career for Roy, it was not without its rewards. Roy won his first feature race at Jefferson Speedway, and his son/pit crew Matt was there to see it. After

On Sunday afternoons, Matt would root for his favorite NASCAR driver, Dale Earnhardt. Then, father and son would head out to the shop and work on their car. Matt looks back fondly at his career beginnings. "I can still remember working in our little Rockdale shop—smelling the wood stove we used to burn to keep warm. Dad would stand in front of the wood stove while we worked. Mom would cook meals for all of us, and when I needed her to, she would sit in the car while I put

First late model win, June 1988.
(Kenseth family photo)

it on the scales. That was always a good one."

Most of Matt's high school days were not spent at football games or dances; instead they were spent in the little shop near the Kenseths' house. With a few buddies, Matt spent the next several years learning all about his race car—how to build it, how to fix it, how to pay for it, and how to win with it. Matt's dad recalls, "Matt wasn't shy about ordering the best and most expensive parts!" After graduating from Cambridge High School in 1990, Matt continued to live at home and began working as a technical assistant at stock car builder Lefthander Chassis in Rockford, Illinois. His job also included working on some of the cars and doing bodywork. "Working at Lefthander helped a lot, because I learned more every time I worked on something," Matt said. "And when the new stuff came out, I got to see it right away."

His grandpa Helmer remembers Matt's early work habits. "It must have been the second year after Matt got started and I stopped in the shop and he was writing on a notebook, keeping track

(Kenseth family photo)

of things. He said, 'This is my third book already.' He kept records of everything, and that's how he learned how to set up the cars."

Matt continued to call on his experienced uncles for help. His aunt Kathy said, "I can't tell you how many times Matt called for [his uncle] Gary. It was always the same message I gave him: 'Matt called, he needs help setting up his lifters!'"

He continued to compete in as many races as

he could, moving up to the late model division. He won the season opener at Slinger, and finished sixth in the overall point standings that year. That was the beginning of his presence as a winner and points challenger. Money and sponsorship were factors in the amount of races Matt could run. He decided to focus on the ARTGO series, and competed in the Red, White and Blue State Championship Series at Wisconsin International Raceway, and raced in the Miller Nationals at Slinger and their Sunday night points program.

Matt's goals had broadened since the previous year of 1989. Now he was saying, "I want to be a full-time race car driver. It doesn't matter on what circuit or what part of the country. My goal is to drive race cars professionally."

Many writers touted Matt's career proclaiming, "It was never a matter of if he would win a major race, but when." One year later, in April of 1991, Matt stunned the field and won an ARTGO race in his first visit to LaCrosse Fairgrounds. Matt was elated by the win. "I had no idea how many laps were left!" The team did not have the luxury of a two-way radio to communicate with the crew. Matt, only 19, was the youngest driver to win. Suddenly the comparisons began. This youngster sure seemed a lot like the previous record holder, a skinny kid from Batesville, Arkansas, who had taken the Midwest by storm—Mark Martin.

Many writers touted Matt's career proclaiming, "It was never a matter of if he would win a major race, but when."

CHAPTER 5

MANAGING the MIDWEST

> ## " He was a little bit aggressive. He had to be, a little punk kid coming up and trying to take over. "
>
> —*Wisconsin native Steve Strasburg,*
> *stepson of local racing legend Joe Shear*

During the early '90s, Matt Kenseth was becoming a household name in Wisconsin. At the 1990 season opener at Slinger, Matt secured his first late model win. The following week he held off NASCAR Winston Cup driver Ted Musgrave for a second win. He had graduated from the sportsman class to late models and did not seem to be struggling with the transition. In 1991, Matt said goodbye to the Buick body style and secured

Matt, Roy and crewman Todd Millard with an ASA entry in 1995. *(Kenseth family photo)*

" Races are really won at home in the shop, not on the race track. "
—*Matt Kenseth*

sponsorship from his employer, Lefthander Chassis. In addition, Prototype Racing Engines stickers adorned his Chevy Lumina. His car was painted white with a red No. 8. When asked about his early success, he reflected on his timely experience. "I was pretty much the only guy who worked on his [father's] car. When I started racing, I knew what the car was doing and what I needed to do to the car, and that helped a lot. Races are really won at home in the shop, not on the race track. I think my work with the setup is the main thing that helped me." Matt claimed the Rookie of the Year title at Slinger that year, finishing sixth in the overall point standings.

In 1992, bad luck was a costly learning curve for the Kenseths. Engine problems and accidents took Matt's work in the shop to a new level. Racing took up a small portion of time compared to the hundreds of hours spent rebuilding and repairing body damage and engine failures. Even though the

Matt had some fun showering car owner Fred Neilsen at the Miller Genuine Draft Nationals at Madison, WI in July 1994. *(photo by Doug Hornickel)*

extreme maintenance took a toll on Matt's time, the confidence that came from knowing every inch of his race car translated to his skills on the track.

In 1993, Matt won his first feature at WIR (Kaukauna) and captured the track's Rookie of the Year title as well. Matt spent hundreds of laps competing against Robbie Reiser, the Allenton, Wisconsin, driver who was the defending track

champion at Madison International Speedway in 1991 and 1992. Matt's biggest victory of the year was in the Wisconsin Short Track Series finale at Madison, where he passed Reiser for the lead, and completed his winning romp on lap 200. It was worth $5,000 for the All-Car-sponsored team of Matt Kenseth. Although Reiser won the series title, which included the use of an ASA car and a hauler for the 1994 season, Matt finished a respectable sixth in the series. In addition, 1993 brought Matt a fistful of wins at his regular venues of Madison, Slinger, Kaukauna, and impressive ARTGO wins at Norway and LaCrosse.

The 1994 season meant expansion, opportunities and experience for Matt. He and his father continued "Kenseth Racing," fielding their own cars on Friday nights at Madison and Saturday nights at the Dells. Car owners Mike and Patty Butz from Green Bay teamed up with Matt to accomplish their goal of winning the 1994 championship at Wisconsin International Raceway. Furthermore, Matt's mentor and friend, Joe Shear, was leaving Fred Nielsen's Lake Villa operation to field his own team, leaving the door wide open for some lucky driver to slide into this top-sponsored ride. Although many drivers were considered, Matt was at the top of the list and happily accepted the job.

The original plan included 20 to 25 short-track races and five ASA races. The combination proved to be fruitful early on. Matt shared the spotlight

One of Matt's many wins at LaCrosse.
(photo by Doug Hornickel)

with Reiser as each won a 75-lap feature, Matt clinched the fast dash, Robbie was fast qualifier, and Matt won the series title. In July, Matt won his most prestigious title yet—the Miller Genuine

Draft Nationals. Nicknamed "Matt the Brat" for his uncanny knack of driving with experience beyond his years, this performance was proof of his flourishing reputation. Matt competed against NASCAR Winston Cup drivers of the day—Ken Schrader, Dick Trickle, and Rich Bickle—and the Midwest's toughest competition—Butch Miller, Joe Shear, Scott Hansen and Conrad Morgan—and came out on top. He wrapped up track championships in 1994 at both Wisconsin International Raceway and Madison International Speedway, completing 100 percent of the total laps run. In a total of 63 events, Matt scored 57 top-10 finishes, 48 top-five finishes, 23 dash or fast heat wins, and 18 feature event wins, with only six DNFs (did not finish). Matt's statistics proved that his consistency and his demeanor meant more wins and championships in the future.

In 1995, he won races and his second track championship at Kaukauna. He finished second in the points standings at Madison International

Taking home another win at Jefferson Speedway in July, 1992. *(photo by Doug Hornickel)*

39

Madison International Speedway in April, 1993. *(photo by Doug Hornickel)*

Speedway. He found success with Fred Neilsen and competed in a few ASA races, hoping for television coverage. The next logical step was to break into the NASCAR Craftsman Truck Series or secure a full-time ASA ride.

"The end of '95 was kind of a turning point," Matt said. "I was racing for Fred [Neilsen] but couldn't get him to commit to a full ASA deal. My dad and I built a brand new car and bought new shop equipment. We raced a few All-Pro races with our own money in Myrtle Beach, Nashville, Jefferson [Georgia] and Pensacola. We ended up running good, finishing second in one race and a top five in another." But it wasn't quite the direction in which Matt or Roy had hoped to be going. Matt had made his home racing in the Midwest for the last seven years. It was time to turn his direction south.

Matt and Kenny Wallace at the Miller Genuine Nationals in Madison, WI in June, 1995. *(photo by Doug Hornickel)*

"**Oh, yeah. The local Wisconsin thing was always 'Matt the Brat.' He'd get upset.**"

—*Wisconsin native Scott Wimmer of NASCAR's Busch Series, on the nickname given to Kenseth*

CHAPTER 6

MOVING SOUTH

Matt and his ASA ride at Madison Speedway in August, 1995.
(photo by Doug Hornickel)

> ## " I liked Matt from the first time I saw him. I liked the way he handled himself, both on and off the track. I could tell that he was a very talented young man who had a bright future in this sport. "
>
> *—Mark Martin*

I t's not that Matt wasn't content living at home with his parents. But Rockdale just wasn't a mecca for stock car racing. He had covered the field at the Wisconsin tracks, and now he had his hopes set on the southern home of racing, North Carolina. Even though Matt had experienced success in the Midwest, the paychecks always disappeared into more equipment. He was pretty much broke when he loaded up some furniture in his stock car trailer and moved to Huntersville.

"I got an offer from Carl Wegner to move to North Carolina and run the Hooters Cup. Our hope was to move up to the NASCAR Busch Series or NASCAR Craftsman Truck Series full time in 1996. We sold the car that we won the championship with at Madison International [in 1994] and Carl bought the All-Pro car from us." The little shop in Cambridge was without a race car for the first time in ten years.

Matt accepted the offer to run for the Hooters Cup championship, not to mention plans that included select NASCAR All-Pro events and five races in both NASCAR Busch Series and NASCAR Craftsman Truck divisions. Matt held his own against the rough cut of drivers on the Hooters menu, and managed to achieve his first

Tony Raines (87), Matt Kenseth (68) and Bob Senneker (84) at the ASA Badgerland 150, Milwaukee, WI in August 1995.
(photo by Doug Hornickel)

Matt's pensive look started early in his career.
(photo by Doug Hornickel)

victory in Anderson, South Carolina. He finished third in Hooters points. Hooters Cup was a different racing format than what Matt was accustomed to. It was Matt's first time in a traveling series that included pit stops. Matt adjusted and learned.

In May of 1996, Matt made his NASCAR Busch Series debut at Charlotte in an unsponsored car rented from Bobby Dotter. He was satisfied with staying out of trouble and finished 31st. He still entertained hopes of additional NASCAR Busch Series races, but lack of sponsorship and financial hardship forbade it. Running without financial help was much more expensive than he expected.

Despite Matt's determination to put down roots in the South, he was beckoned back to Wisconsin in 1997 by Gerry Gunderman. Gunderman owned a well-established ASA team, and Matt was ready for a full-time shot at the ASA circuit. He relocated to Milwaukee and began building cars. Their first outing was in Kenly, North Carolina, where Matt finished second. Before Matt left the track that night, he received a career-changing phone call.

CHAPTER 7

FRIENDLY RIVALS

Some of the headlines in '93 looked like this: "Kenseth Nets Race," "Reiser Gets Title," "Kenseth Tops Reiser in Wisconsin Short Track Series Finale," "Kenseth Holds off Reiser," "Kenseth Wins Wisconsin Short Track Series Final," and "Reiser is Series King." Robbie and Matt's relationship on the track was purely competitive. They were both there to win. While competing in the WSTS, during the season finale

> "There's no question that Matt Kenseth is a great driver...this is a great team, and they got it all together right now."
>
> —*Robbie Reiser*

Miller Genuine Draft Nationals winner Matt Kenseth
celebrates at Madison International Speedway
in July, 1994. *(photo by Doug Hornickel)*

Kenseth won his first 200-lap race and Reiser scored the series title. While Reiser's title earned him the use of an ASA car and hauler for the '94 season, Robbie's sights were set higher on NASCAR Busch Series racing. It would be another three years before Kenseth and Reiser would join forces, leave their rivalry behind in Wisconsin, and remain in alliance for years to come.

Reiser struggled on a limited budget and began to compete part-time in the NASCAR Busch Series. Soon after he saw racing as a business, Robbie realized acting as crew chief and driver was time consuming and nearly impossible. He opted for crew chief, and in 1997 secured a driver, Tim Bender, and a full-time sponsor in Kraft Singles. After Bender suffered a neck injury in Bristol, Kenseth found himself the recipient of a surprising phone call. Robbie's decision to call had been based on their past competition. Matt had been riding out the Wisconsin weather in an ASA ride with Gerry Gunderman and now faced a troubling decision. Reiser was offering a six-race deal, maybe enough to get Matt noticed on the NASCAR circuit, but it meant walking away from a commitment and a promising season in ASA. After weighing his options, Matt again turned his prospects south.

Matt's first appearance with the team was at Nashville Speedway. He qualified third and finished 11th. The next race was his first superspeedway start. Matt finished seventh at Talladega. In July, the team returned to their home state of Wisconsin to the Milwaukee Mile. Matt suffered a potentially dangerous crash at the one-mile venue. During the morning practice, the throttle stuck. He took a path straight for the wall. Luckily Matt was not injured. The team qualified with a backup car, finishing a respectable 12th. Matt's best finishes that year were placing third at both Dover and California.

As the season drew to a close, Kraft Singles announced they would not be returning in 1998.

Matt and Robbie Reiser with the Kraft Singles backup car at the Milwaukee Mile, July 1997. *(photo by Doug Hornickel)*

MATT KENSETH

ABOVE AND BEYOND

(photo by Doug Hornickel)

Even though the team's financial future hung in the balance, Matt found Robbie knowledgeable and easy to talk to. Robbie's experience as a driver helped cement this new relationship between crew chief and driver. They completed the 1997 season with two top fives and seven top tens, and a second-place finish in the Rookie of the Year standings.

Matt makes a pit stop in the Milwaukee Mile in 1997, he would finish the season 22nd in points in the NASCAR Busch series. *(photo by Doug Hornickel)*

(photo by Doug Hornickel)

CHAPTER 8

A PROTÉGÉ and HIS MENTOR

It's hard to say just what caught Mark Martin's eye. The comparisons began when Matt erased Mark's name from the record books with the ARTGO win in 1990. They also shared a history of racing many of the same tracks in the Midwest. More importantly, Mark, mentored by Wisconsin legend Dick Trickle, had also unsuccessfully tried to enter into the NASCAR Busch Series, only to be plagued with financial problems and an eventual retreat to ASA. Or maybe Mark noticed the same thing many others saw in Matt—unbridled talent. "I guess he likes the way I drive," Matt said. "It's a little overwhelming to be working with him. Mark is someone I always looked up to."

Martin approached Kenseth after a NASCAR Busch Series drivers' meeting at Talladega early in the spring of '97 with an offer to test with him later that year at Darlington. Matt was surprised, this

Eventual winner Mark Martin (60) leads Jeff Burton (9) who finished third and Matt (17) who took second place at Darlington in 2000. *(photo by Doug Hornickel)*

> **"I've been wrong about a lot of things in my life, but I was right about Matt Kenseth. I'm real proud of that."**
>
> —*Mark Martin*

being only his second NASCAR Busch Series start, and talking with Mark Martin about his future. It was here that Matt had his first opportunity in a NASCAR Winston Cup car, and where the beginnings of a solid friendship with Martin began. When that day came, Matt found himself chatting about chassis setups with Mark, while running some non-record-breaking speed laps at the "Lady in Black." By the time Matt's first season in the NASCAR Busch Series concluded, he had secured a "five-year testing contract" with Roush Racing, which had also taken an interest in helping Reiser Enterprises and Matt secure a NASCAR Busch Series sponsorship for 1998. Mark continued to be pivotal in Matt's career for the next several years, speaking up for the budding star and opening the door for endless learning opportunities.

In the early days, Matt felt more like a Mark Martin fan than a future teammate. On one breakfast outing, Matt remembers that Mark couldn't finish his breakfast. "Mark couldn't even eat his eggs. There were so many people looking at him, and coming up to talk to him." Mark began to influence Matt in off-track practices, teaching him the importance of a regimented physical workout and eating only healthy food. Mark's son Matt was competitive in go-kart racing and Matt's son Ross was just starting out. They were never at a loss for something to talk about.

> **"I guess he likes the way I drive. It's a little overwhelming to be working with him. Mark is someone I always looked up to."**
>
> *—Matt Kenseth*

Mark Martin and Matt talk strategy before a NASCAR Busch Series race in 2000. (photo by Doug Hornickel)

(photo by Doug Hornickel)

Mark's wisdom sometimes took the form of humor toward Matt. When Matt bumped Mark off the pole for a NASCAR Busch Series race in Atlanta, Mark called his lap "young and dumb." Mark went on to win the race, but Matt finished second—the only car even close to challenging Mark for the win.

Mark Martin was (and still is) listed as car owner, along with Jack Roush, when Matt took the DeWALT Tools-sponsored Ford Taurus for its five scheduled runs in 1999. The fall schedule included Michigan, Darlington, Dover, Charlotte and Rockingham, which was Matt's final practice before bidding for NASCAR Winston Cup Rookie of the Year honors in 2000.

Although Mark always remained a mentor and teacher, his intensity toward his own racing career eventually limited the time Mark and Matt were able to spend together.

" **He is a great friend and has been a tremendous influence on my career, but if we're both racing for the win I'm gonna try my best to beat him – just like Mark is going to do his best to beat me. If he wins, I'll be the first to shake his hand, hug his neck, and congratulate him.** "

—Matt Kenseth on his relationship with Mark Martin

CHAPTER 9

A BUSCH SERIES BREAKTRHOUGH

> **"Momentum is the most underrated thing in all of sports. That, and Robbie Reiser."**
> —*Ryan Smithson*

The 1998 season began with one goal—to win races. Matt would compete in the 31-race NASCAR Busch Series schedule. In Daytona, Reiser Enterprises was prepared to announce its primary sponsor when the whole deal fell apart. It looked like the end of the road until a midnight meeting secured Lycos, an Internet search engine, for a one-race deal. A day before the race, a NASCAR official accompanied Reiser's Chevrolet

Matt, Robbie and Tony Stewart compare notes prior to the start of a race at the Milwaukee Mile in 1998. *(photo by Doug Hornickel)*

" Matt Kenseth—oh my gosh—he's good. "

—Randy LaJoie

out of the track to have it painted black and to have the decals applied. Despite their sixth-place finish at Daytona, the next week at Rockingham the blue-and-red car with a yellow 17 sported only a small Lycos decal on its rear quarter panel. The decal was a thank you and perhaps enticement into further sponsorship. Throughout the running of the Goodwrench Service Plus 200, the driver of the 1998 Chevy was referred to several times as "Robbie Reiser," but in the last few laps there was no confusion as to who was driving. Matt gave a dramatic bump to Tony Stewart's left rear, which caused Tony to be bumped up and out of the groove, opening the door for Matt. Crossing the finish line was a monumental occasion for both Robbie and Matt. The 25-year-old Midwesterner from Cambridge, Wisconsin, with only 24

NASCAR Busch Series starts, came out on top. He stood on top of his unsponsored car with a logo-free blue drivers' suit and the points lead. Matt was ecstatic. Tony was not. "You've got to do what you've got to do," Matt reported.

Matt's dad was there to relish his son's first

Matt and Roy after Matt's first career NASCAR Busch Series win at Rockingham, NC. *(Kenseth family photo)*

"You've got to do what you've got to do."
—Matt Kenseth

A four-tire pit stop and fuel for the car, bottle of water for the driver in 1998. *(photo by Doug Hornickel)*

> **“Matt is a superstar in the making. He is a tremendous driver and if somebody said, ‘Why don’t you create from scratch the ultimate race car driver?’ That’s the one. ”**
>
> —*Mark Martin*

victory. When Roy returned to Cambridge, there were hand-painted signs in business windows and "Congratulations Matt" lettered on the bank marquee.

Mark Martin finished third and congratulated Matt in victory lane. Mark later paid Matt the ultimate compliment when asked a question about their relationship during an online chat. He said, "Matt is a superstar in the making. He is a tremendous driver and if somebody said, 'Why don't you create from scratch the ultimate race car driver?' That's the one." When two-time NASCAR Busch Series Champion Randy LaJoie was asked to name his competition for an upcoming race at Darlington he mentioned Mark Martin, Jeff Burton and Tony Stewart. But he went on to say, "Matt Kenseth—oh my gosh—he's good." Matt basked in the glory of his victory—it was hard earned.

A few weeks later, Lycos signed on as the primary sponsor for the remainder of the season. It was only a few months later that they began to reap big dividends. On June 14, Matt started on the pole, won his second NASCAR Busch Series race, the Lycos.com 250 at Pikes Peak International Raceway, and regained the series points lead.

(photo by Doug Hornickel)

CHAPTER 10

A COMPETITIVE FIELD

Competition in the NASCAR Busch Series was at a peak. Steve Park, 1997's Rookie of the Year, had fared well as a newcomer, and had also raised the bar for future performances by Tony Stewart, Dale Earnhardt Jr. and Matt Kenseth. Seasoned veterans like Randy LaJoie, Elton Sawyer, Mike McLaughlin and Todd Bodine, along with NASCAR Winston Cup regulars Mark Martin, Bobby Labonte and Jeff Burton, kept the competition lively. But by the end of 1998, the NASCAR Busch Series had become Matt Kenseth vs. Dale Earnhardt Jr. The two had become friends, and there was rarely an interview or article that didn't mention the two synonymously. Additionally, they were door to door or fender to fender in most of the NASCAR Busch Series races. As the 1998 season began to wind down, Junior was in the points lead, and Matt was in heated pursuit. After race

Matt and Dale Jr. enjoyed some very lively competition in their NASCAR Busch series racing days.
(photo by Doug Hornickel)

66 **Well, it depends upon how you define it. I mean, we're good friends. But we both want to beat each other....** 99

—Matt Kenseth on his relationship with Dale Jr.

ABOVE AND BEYOND

(photo by Doug Hornickel)

number 31, Matt posted three wins, 17 top fives and 22 top tens but fell 48 points short of champion Dale Jr.

The 1999 season opened up fresh possibilities with a rematch with Dale Jr. and a new sponsor, DeWALT Tools. Ironically, Matt's first NASCAR Busch Series win of the year came at Darlington in March. A NASCAR Winston Cup stand-in job for injured Bobby Labonte followed that Sunday. Helmer recalls, "When Bobby Labonte got hurt and couldn't run, he said, 'Get Matt Kenseth, he never wrecks cars.' Matt had to jump in the car under a caution after Bobby started and dropped back to 40th place. Matt made it all the way up to tenth before it got rained out."

Matt and Junior remained neck and neck throughout the season. Jeff Green was also becoming a strong contender. The media continued to surround the son of Dale Earnhardt and his greatest challenger. As their relationship on the track heated up, tempers flared when Junior wrecked a dominant Kenseth at Dover. Their

Matt and Kenny Wallace on a hot July day in 1999. *(photo by Doug Hornickel)*

Matt and Robbie going over last-minute strategy.
(photo by Doug Hornickel)

schedules were filled with interviews, appearances and the newly found responsibilities associated with making the move to NASCAR Winston Cup. Dale Jr. was fast becoming NASCAR's bad boy, while Matt appeared to be more stable and mellow. Despite a mutual respect for each other, their days of "hanging out" were diminishing.

By September, their statistics were nearly a mirror image, each driver claiming 17 top tens, 13

Once again Matt and Dale Jr. are neck and neck in a NASCAR Busch series race. *(photo by Doug Hornickel)*

top fives, with the only difference being that Junior edged by with five wins to Matt's four. Twenty-six points separated the two from a championship. As the year slowly rolled past, Matt faded. The final race of the year at Homestead, Dale Jr. had already clinched the title just by starting the race. Matt and Jeff Green battled for second, but Matt blew a motor and settled for a third-place finish in the NASCAR Busch Series Championship in 1999.

> " When Bobby Labonte got hurt and couldn't run, he said, 'Get Matt Kenseth, he never wrecks cars.' "
> —*Helmer Kenseth*

CHAPTER 11

AN UNEXPECTED DEBUT

(photo by Jim Garrahan)

MATT KENSETH

> ## " He's just really smart, kept really calm and cool. He just did a great job. "
> —*Joe Garone*

Moments after Matt cashed in his third NASCAR Busch Series victory at Dover in 1998, he jumped into a NASCAR Winston Cup car. He had been testing NASCAR Winston Cup cars for months with Mark Martin, but this was neither a Roush Ford nor a test. It was Happy Hour—the final NASCAR Winston Cup practice for the MBNA Gold 400 scheduled for Sunday. Bill Elliott's father had passed away the previous day and Martin suggested Matt as a

replacement. Crew chief Joe Garone and team manager Mike Beam had not even met Matt. However, less than 24 hours later, they were communicating like a veteran team. Matt qualified 16th, ran in the top five most of the day, and at one point was in second place behind the eventual race winner Mark Martin. Matt recalls, "The only time I got emotional was when I passed Rusty Wallace. Mark was the only car in front of me. Then I got a little goofy for a few laps and thought about catching him."

Matt was colorful in every way that Sunday. Elliott's McDonald's Ford was sporting a special tie-dye Big Mac paint scheme and a matching driver's suit. Matt was right in the sponsor groove when radio traffic picked up this conversation with crew chief Garone. Garone asked his driver what he needed during an upcoming pit stop. Matt replied, "I need some water, don't need any adjustments on the car—and hold the fries." On another humorous exchange, Matt smoked the tires leaving pit road and radioed in, "Sorry for the John

Force exit boys."

It was quite a change for Matt who spent most of his Sundays on the couch watching NASCAR Winston Cup races. When asked about possibly being intimidated by the NASCAR Winston Cup regulars, Matt replied, "I'm a racer. I race as hard as I can. That's just the way I'm built, and that's the way I was raised." The praise was unanimous from fellow drivers and teams. Rusty Wallace referred to Matt as "talented and smooth," and Joe Garone said, "He's just really smart, kept really calm and cool. He just did a great job." The media attention carried over into the next day. Matt's phone rang continually with congratulations and job offers from car owners. Despite the persuasiveness of the offers, Matt remained loyal to mentor Mark Martin and his contract with Roush Racing.

Matt's sixth-place finish was the best debut performance by a driver in a NASCAR Winston Cup Series race since Rusty Wallace finished second at Atlanta on March 3, 1980.

> " David Pearson always moved around with a low profile. He did his talking on the racetrack. I mean, David talked to people. But he didn't always come up with a catchy quote or something that would make a headline. And Kenseth is the same way. "
>
> —*Jim Hunter*

"The only time I got emotional was when I passed Rusty Wallace. Mark was the only car in front of me. Then I got a little goofy for a few laps and thought about catching him. "

—*Matt Kenseth*

(photo by Jim Garrahan)

CHAPTER 12

MAKING the MOVE to WINSTON CUP

M att Kenseth now had two years of solid NASCAR Busch Series experience after completing the 1998 and 1999 seasons. Jack Roush said he expected Matt to finish in the top five in points and to win a race during his rookie year in the NASCAR Winston Cup Series. Mark Martin also expected Matt to do well. Mark deserved a lot of credit for getting Matt started. After his impressive run in Elliott's car, Mark said,

Matt and his son, Ross, enjoy some father-son time in 1999.
(photo by Doug Hornickel)

> ## " **Everybody's going to be after him now, and I think it's kind of funny because he just isn't available. "**
> —*Mark Martin*

"Everybody's going to be after him now, and I think it's kind of funny because he just isn't available."

Matt expressed his loyalties to Mark and Jack early on. "Mark told me, 'Just remember who is giving you the start and who is giving you the break.' I will never forget that, and I will do whatever Mark thinks we should do as long as he is interested in me and wants to help me."

Matt was relieved to know that Robbie would make the move with him to the NASCAR Winston Cup Series. Robbie's ownership and involvement in Reiser Enterprises and the NASCAR Busch Series team remained his most important goal, but

as long as Matt would still race a partial NASCAR Busch Series schedule, Robbie could relinquish some of his control to a new crew chief and graduate to the ranks of the NASCAR Winston Cup Series full time in 2000. For the 1999 season's five NASCAR Winston Cup races, Robbie would test the waters in his new career as crew chief.

Matt adjusted fairly well to the media circus that surrounded him. Only a few years ago, his entire crew consisted of his father and a few guys helping out. Now he maintained relationships with two full-time crews, two car owners, and off-track friendships with other drivers. "It's hard for me at

(Kenseth family photo)

Matt and Robbie in their rookie year of NASCAR Winston Cup Racing.
(photo by Doug Hornickel)

MATT KENSETH

> 66 **Mark told me, 'Just remember who is giving you the start and who is giving you the break.' I will never forget that, and I will do whatever Mark thinks we should do as long as he is interested in me and wants to help me.** 99
>
> *—Matt Kenseth*

(photo by Doug Hornickel)

times to keep up with all of it. I just do the best I can."

"The hardest thing was getting used to the routine," Matt said about Sunday racing. There was so much new information. "For Robbie, it was learning how tech works. For me, it was just learning how to get in and out of the garage area, and getting to know the officials, other crews and other competitors." Besides trying to fit in and getting used to seeing new people every week, there was the matter of Sundays. "Sunday used to be a fun day. Everyone [the crew and Robbie] would get together and watch the race on TV, cook out, jet ski, and go out on the boat." For Matt, Sundays would still be fun, just in a less relaxing sort of way.

Wisconsin legend Dick Trickle (14) and Matt Kenseth (17) at Darlington. *(photo by Doug Hornickel)*

CHAPTER **13**

ROOKIE of the YEAR

> **"I'm so happy for Matt and Robbie. They are a class act. We became good friends with those guys the last two seasons in the Busch series. I know how hard they work at it, and they deserve it."**
>
> —*Dale Jr. on Matt winning Rookie of the Year honors in 2000*

MATT KENSETH

Not surprisingly Matt and Junior were logical candidates for NASCAR Winston Cup Rookie of the Year honors.
(photo by Doug Hornickel)

The year 2000 was one of young guns waiting to make their marks on the veterans of NASCAR's premier division. Seven rookies contended for the NASCAR Winston Cup Rookie of the Year title and everyone looked to the son of a legend to walk away with it. Tony Stewart had outlived all expectations with three wins in his rookie season in 1999. Now the rookie class of 2000 was under pressure to win right out of the box.

Matt chose, in addition to running a full NASCAR Winston Cup schedule, to continue to race in the NASCAR Busch Series. Visine had joined forces with Reiser Enterprises and a 20-race schedule had been assembled with some of the previous NASCAR Busch Series crewmen and a new crew chief. Matt used four fresh tires as pit strategy and drafting help from Joe Nemechek to cement his first win at Daytona and create a record three top-ten finishes in three starts. It was Matt's eighth NASCAR Busch Series win in 86 races.

Matt's DEWALT team was sound, with Robbie Reiser as crew chief and several of the NASCAR Busch Series crewmen moving up to the NASCAR Winston Cup Series, along with the previous two years of experience, the team was beginning to earn dividends. Teammates Jeff Burton, Mark Martin and the rest of the gang at Roush were contributing as well. However, when Dale Jr. won his first NASCAR Winston Cup race at Texas and then duplicated his efforts at Richmond, the pressure to win became ever present.

Matt took advantage of the Burton brothers' late race spins in Fontana to chalk up his second NASCAR Busch Series victory of the year. The following Sunday, it looked as if he, too, would pick up his first NASCAR Winston Cup win at California. After leading more than 100 laps and dominating the second half of the race, a late race caution shook up the field and squelched his bid for victory. Matt was disappointed, "I sat there all day and planned on losing, because I just knew something was going to happen. The minute we were home free, sure enough, there was the yellow." The consistent Reiser and Kenseth chose to take four tires instead of two and were mired too deep in traffic to reclaim a higher position than third. Jeremy Mayfield won, but Matt came out of the shadows, proving to be more of a threat to win now than ever.

Coming into Charlotte in May, Matt and Junior were both running in the top 15 in points and competitively performing each week. Dale Jr. turned heads and had crowds roaring with his free-for-all victory at The Winston, where he picked up the pole position for Sunday night's Coca-Cola 600. But the "other rookie" would shine in NASCAR's longest race.

However, when Dale Jr. won his first Cup race at Texas and then duplicated his efforts at Richmond, the pressure to win became ever present.

There's that pensive look again.
(photo by Doug Hornickel)

MATT KENSETH

Matt battles for position with his boyhood idol, Dale Earnhardt at Darlington in 2000. *(photo by Doug Hornickel)*

CHAPTER 14

RAIN DELAY

Most NASCAR drivers make their homes in the Charlotte, North Carolina area. Midseason they settle down to spend a good chunk of time at Lowe's Motor Speedway in Concord. After The Winston weekend, qualifying and practices stretch from Wednesday through Saturday. Sunday night is a long time coming, but the atmosphere under the lights with 185,000 fans all waiting to spend their nights with screaming tires

> **"My heart started beating pretty hard as soon as I took the lead from Bobby. "**
>
> —*Matt Kenseth*

and revving engines gives it an alluring flavor.

The night was rainy, halting the race partway through and holding it up for about an hour. But the crowd waited and watched bids for the lead as Dale Jr. and Jerry Nadeau both ran well early that evening. Nadeau had engine problems and Dale Jr. had pit stop problems. Fortunately, Matt Kenseth had no problems. "My heart started beating pretty hard as soon as I took the lead from Bobby," recalls Matt. Running a clean and smart race, the last laps were ticking off as Matt glanced in his rearview mirror. It was still full of Bobby Labonte, one of the Winston No Bull competitors who would receive an additional $1 million for a win. Tonight it was Matt's turn. When he crossed the finish line, flash bulbs flickered, fans cheered, the DeWALT pit crew went airborne from the pit wall, and a 28-year-old rookie driver who was not

(photo by Doug Hornickel)

> " I can't believe how good the racecar was. I was using the tires up pretty hard to keep Bobby behind me. I didn't know if he was saving his car or not, but I was going as hard as I could. "
>
> —*Matt Kenseth*

a good ol' boy and was not Dale Jr. elated everyone with his stunning win. Seconds later the DEWALT Ford tore through the infield grass, spraying water and sod in true celebratory style. When Matt got out of his car to face the press, he could not hide his emotion. A win at Charlotte in his 18th career start. How did he pull it off? By racing the same way he does every race, every week. "I can't believe how good the race car was. I was using the tires up pretty hard to keep Bobby behind me. I didn't know if he was saving his car or not, but I was going as hard as I could," Matt told reporters. In victory lane, Matt was joined by his fiancée Katie, crew chief Reiser, Mark Martin, Jack Roush and later was doused with a bottle of water by Dale Jr. The DEWALT crew had been redeemed after their struggles the previous week during The Winston. Their pit stops were flawless. Diligence had paid off. In addition to the excitement of the win, Matt remained in the points lead in the rookie battle. Although Junior had more wins, Matt was becoming known for his consistency. Matt had

(photo by Doug Hornickel)

(photo by Doug Hornickel)

come from a 21st-place qualifying effort to win NASCAR's longest race. He was the only driver outside the top 20, not to mention the only rookie to date, to clinch a Coca-Cola 600.

Matt continued to mow down the competition in the NASCAR Busch Series, winning back-to-back races at Dover and Charlotte. Double duty, racing in both NASCAR Busch Series and NASCAR Winston Cup Series is more than a full-time job. But Matt methodically ran his races as his first full season in NASCAR Winston Cup drew to a close. He had not relinquished his lead in the rookie battle. Just like math class, the rookie point system is just a little harder than it has to be. Even though Matt had more points, NASCAR still had the right to award the title to a competitor, based on wins, on- and off-track attitude and the like. Since Dale Jr. had been the obvious favorite, Kenseth fans held their breath and waited to see if Matt would receive this prestigious award.

In December 2000, Matt attended his first NASCAR Winston Cup Banquet in New York and

He was the
only driver outside
the top 20, not to
mention the only
rookie to date,
to clinch a
Coca-Cola 600.

(photo by Kelley Maruszewski)

was presented with the Raybestos Rookie of the Year Award and a check for $50,000. Matt's season in comparison may not have been as exciting as Dale Jr.'s victorious romps, but Matt's level-headed, steady-handed season was a victory as well.

Matt capped off his year by marrying his best friend, Katie Martin. The two had met at a mutual friend's wedding, and had been together ever since. Matt and Katie were married in Wisconsin, and then a few weeks later made an appearance at the Matt Kenseth Fan Club's first annual party. More than 1,000 fans turned out to congratulate Matt on his Raybestos Rookie of the Year title and recent marriage.

MATT KENSETH

Matt and Katie spend a few minutes together before race time. *(photo by Doug Hornickel)*

CHAPTER 15

SOPHOMORE STRUGGLES

Rich Bickle (59) and Matt Kenseth (17) fight for position in the NASCAR Busch series in 2001. *(photo by Doug Hornickel)*

As the countdown to Daytona 2001 began, the spotlight again shone on Matt and Dale Earnhardt Jr., this year pitted against each other as potential NASCAR Winston Cup champs. Rookies Casey Atwood, Kurt Busch and Jason Leffler were hard-pressed to achieve the friendly rivalry and celebrity status that the previous year's candidates possessed. Matt would again pull double duty, racing 20 NASCAR Busch Series races in addition

(photo by Doug Hornickel)

to his full NASCAR Winston Cup schedule. The DEWALT car sported a special all-yellow paint scheme with the Raybestos Rookie of the Year logo emblazoned on the hood. However as the 2001 season began, NASCAR history would forever be changed when, on the last lap of the Daytona 500, Dale Earnhardt's Chevrolet slammed head on into the outside retaining wall of the Speedway. A few hours later, a dark cloud again settled over the NASCAR community as the news came that Earnhardt had not survived the crash. Matt had always known that in the game of high speed and chance, danger lurked in the shadows. It could have been anybody. It could have been him.

Despite low spirits the following week at

Matt had always known that in the game of high speed and chance, danger lurked in the shadows. It could have been anybody. It could have been him.

MATT KENSETH

(photo by Doug Hornickel)

Rockingham, 43 drivers started their engines. The atmosphere in the garage area of the tight-knit community was closer than ever. Each driver and crewmember honored the memory of Dale with a black hat bearing the familiar No. 3. Dale Jr.'s life and career would take a decidedly different turn, and finally a distinction forged between the comparative paths of Matt and Junior.

(photo by Doug Hornickel)

Dale Jr. went on to have a banner year, winning restrictor plate races and finishing eighth in points. Troubles plagued Matt and the DEWALT team, from blown engines to broken rear end gears. In Atlanta, one of Matt's favorite tracks, the motor blew and sent Matt hard into the wall. The car was engulfed in flames. Matt made a quick exit, able to effortlessly release himself from the now-required HANS safety device. Goodyear came out with a much harder tire, and the team's inability to compensate for its handling differences only added to their problems.

As if that wasn't enough, bad luck and bad weather also affected the team. They used 11 provisionals, and their average starting position was 27.8. Matt was vocal about his disappointment in being unable to run up front and contend for wins. Rumors were beginning to surface about an unsatisfied Matt leaving Roush. It was a hard year.

Near the end of the season, Matt's luck began to turn around, and he posted three fourth-place finishes in the last six races. In October, the DEWALT pit crew won the World Pit Crew Championship at Rockingham, breaking the old record with a 17.695 second stop. Morale began to improve, and Matt statistically finished one position better (13th) in the final point standings than he had the previous year. Matt's final NASCAR Busch Series standings were impressive with one win at Bristol, six second-place finishes, 12 top fives and 14 top tens out of the 24 races that he competed in.

> **"Consistency is the key to finishing well in the points standings, and it's what championships are built upon."**
>
> *—Matt Kenseth*

CHAPTER 16

UNDER the HOOD and OVER the WALL

Roy Kenseth gives a thumbs up on race day.
(photo by Doug Hornickel)

Team 17 is pretty well known. Most pit crews have bright uniforms, but not all of them have the over-the-wall speed and style of the DeWALT crew. Longtime members Mike Calinoff, Jeff Vandermoss, Todd Millard and Russ Strupp all began working with the NASCAR Busch Series team and moved up to the NASCAR Winston Cup Series with Matt in 2000. Todd has the longest record with Matt, volunteering on his crew in the

Midwest since the early '90s. When Matt made the move to the South, Todd was his roommate. Other Wisconsin friends and family joined the crew, including Matt's brother-in-law, Justin Nottestad, who is a front-tire carrier, Matt's cousin, Steve Kenseth, who is pit support on race day, and Todd's brother, Matt Millard, who is pit support as well. Working on a NASCAR Winston Cup crew is a full-time job. Every crewmember has a shop duty Monday through Friday at the Concord race shop. Then they travel to the track for their weekend hours. Winning a race is additional overtime with crewmembers remaining with the winning car three to four hours after the race for inspection. The job description includes plenty of flight time, hotel stays and meals out, but not a lot of time for sightseeing. The garage opens around 6 or 7 a.m. and crews are among the first to arrive. After spending days preparing the cars for the track, they spend the weekends making their shop time pay off. After making adjustments for qualifying, they begin changing over to race setup. Happy Hour consists of a handful of laps run on the track, then into the garage for more adjustments. Although the high-profile pit stops are what most pit crews are noted for, 99 percent of their time is spent working on the car outside of that 14-second window.

The crew seems the most relaxed on Sunday morning. The DeWALT hauler is home to an early-morning team meeting. Brent Swim, truck driver, pit support, and most importantly, the grill man, serves up an early lunch for about 20. In the hours before driver introductions and the green flag, equipment is double checked and transferred to the pit stall and organized. It's not quite a bird's-eye view for the crew. While fans can see much of the track, Jumbotrons and scoreboards, the crew catches their live action on the front stretch. They monitor the race by watching the television mounted in the pit box. When the caution comes out or it's time for a green flag stop, the crew is poised and ready on the wall. After hours of practice every week, this live performance is the only one that counts. The slightest adjustment or the smallest error can cost seconds. Seconds gained or lost in the pits directly translate to seconds gained or lost on the track. But the DeWALT crew more often than not pulls off professional, practiced stops.

Pit road remains a colorful spectacle of speed and smoke.

(photo by Doug Hornickel)

MATT KENSETH

PIT CREW HIGHS and LOWS

- Rockingham 2001: The DEWALT Crew breaks the record with a 17.695-second pit stop and beats 43 other teams for the title of World Championship Pit Crew.

- Charlotte 2002: Matt and his crew pocketed $50,000 for winning the pole position for The Winston with a blistering 13.23-second pit stop.

- Rockingham 2002: The DEWALT Crew won the 76 Unocal World Pit Crew Competition for the second year in a row. They pulled off a 16.832-second pit stop, shattering their previous world record and winning $40,000. The last time the pit crew competition was won in back-to-back years was from 1985-1988 with Dale Earnhardt's crew.

- Contributed to five wins in 2002, consistently getting Matt out in the lead and picking up positions in the pits.

(photo by Doug Hornickel)

CHAPTER 17

FAN FOLLOWING

A trip to any NASCAR race is an assault on the senses. That doesn't mean just the olfactory senses either. While you can rest assured that there are plenty of odors to sample—everything from burning rubber to high octane, and hot dogs to beer, don't overlook all of the visual sights there are. Fans cover themselves from head to toe in apparel and accessories to show support for their favorite drivers. A broad look at the stands and

black, red and orange are sure to be found in the crowd. Ever notice that growing amount of yellow?

Matt's fan base started locally, as most do. Family, friends and fellow racers are sure to show their support early on. In 1997 when Matt was entering into the NASCAR Busch Series, the Internet was becoming the favored mode of information. Two men from Cambridge, Chris Gullickson and Jim Warren approached Roy about using the web address ***www.mattkenseth.com*** and making their growing site of Kenseth articles and photos the "official" Matt Kenseth web site. Six years later with the help of Tennessee web woman Rae Augenstein, they completely maintain a site visited by 40,000 fans daily. About the same time, Roy began to get requests about Matt's fan club. Matt didn't have a fan club. So Roy would clunk out a page or two on his typewriter about his recent travels with his son, handwriting the addresses of a hundred or so people and drop them in the mail.

There probably wasn't much conversation about the NASCAR Busch Series among Cambridge folks until Matt and Dale Jr. began to put on an interesting weekly show. And by the time Matt entered into NASCAR Winston Cup, local appearances were yielding hundreds of fans and requests for fan club memberships. DeWALT merchandise became

(photo by Doug Hornickel)

a full-time business for the Kenseth family.

Matt continues to gain fans from all over the United States and other countries. A fan from Japan sends the Kenseth family a box of gifts every time Matt wins a race. Since Operation Iraqi Freedom began, members of the armed forces have written to request updates on Matt's progress and to show their support for him.

At Matt's first fan club party, he tirelessly signed autographs for more than six hours, smiling for photos. He was genuinely amazed at the fans who turned out for the event. A Wisconsin cake artist comes to all the fan club parties and crafts a cake in 1/10th scale to replicate Matt's current DEWALT ride. Others dedicate walls or rooms in their homes to display their Kenseth memorabilia. Matt

Matt poses with Chelse Lindenbaum and Taylor Bogard at his Annual Fan Club dinner in 2002.
(photo by David Bogard)

remembers one time he was out for a motorcycle ride near his parents' home in Rockdale and rode by a guy fishing who was wearing a DEWALT Racing hat. "That was pretty cool," Matt said. "But it's still kind of weird seeing my name on a hat."

In 2002, a group of 125 fans organized a road trip to Richmond where they began by hanging out at the DEWALT Rolling Thunder display, they then visited the souvenir rig where Joe and Debbey travel the entire NASCAR circuit selling Matt's merchandise. Finally, they sat together to watch Matt win under the lights! The group had members from California, Pennsylvania, Tennessee, Delaware and Canada with one thing in common—their favorite driver is Matt Kenseth.

(photo by Kelley Maruszewski)

(photo by Kelley Maruszewski)

A Wisconsin cake artist comes to all the fan club parties and crafts a cake in 1/10th scale to replicate Matt's current DEWALT ride.

(photo by Doug Hornickel)

Six years later with the help of Tennessee web woman Rae Augenstein, they completely maintain a site visited by 40,000 fans daily.

MATT KENSETH

A banner began circulating in 2001 that became a conversation piece among Matt's fans. It has become a tradition to pass the banner among them, bringing it to every trackside appearance that he makes. Fans wearing Kenseth apparel could sign the banner alongside the DEWALT crew and Matt's signatures. Some fans go by Internet chat names like Kensethaholic, kidkenseth and mattfan17.

Local support remains overwhelming. The parking lots are filled with cars with No. 17 license plates and stickers. It's not uncommon to see a lawnmower or golf cart detailed in the current DEWALT paint scheme. The Cambridge Fire Department erected a 16-by-16 square foot No. 17 on top of the station and adds checkered flags every time Matt wins a race.

Would Richard Petty have signed that first autograph if he'd known it would reach this type of demand? Like most drivers, Matt can't walk more than a few steps in the garage area without giving his Sharpie a workout. Matt signs hats, shirts, pictures, and die-cast cars. He's happy to do it. After all, these are his fans.

Matt's sister Kelley and mom Nicki catch up with Matt at a Wisconsin appearance. *(photo by Doug Hornickel)*

CHAPTER 18

FIVE TIMES VICTORIOUS

(photo by Doug Hornickel)

Momentum. That's what every driver strives for. It's the force that pulls the best out of the previous year, and plugs it into the brain when encouragement is needed. The DeWALT team was oozing with momentum, and they were fired up and ready to get back into racing. Daytona is a wild card, and sure enough Matt was caught up in the "big one." He began his season with a 33rd-place finish, and 33rd in NASCAR

(photo by Doug Hornickel)

Winston Cup Series points. The following week at Rockingham, Matt qualified 25th and showed strength early in the race. He led laps, gained positions in the pits, and was running a smart race. The track surface at Rockingham is a tire shredder. Even after just a few laps on stickered tires, lap times can fall off nearly a full second. When a late race caution flew, Ricky Craven stayed out on old tires, and the leaders Labonte, Marlin and Kenseth all pitted. When the laps were coming to a close, Marlin and Labonte both slid up the track, and Matt made the winning pass inside them both. A spin brought out the last caution flag of the day, and while cleanup ensued, the red flag was not

(photo by Doug Hornickel)

MATT KENSETH

thrown and Matt took the checkered under the yellow. It was a huge win for the DEWALT team. They had been down, but they would not be beaten. Matt had taken himself a piece of "The Rock" as he had done four years ago in his first NASCAR Busch Series victory.

The fanfare died down, and later that evening Matt and his wife flew back to Wisconsin to be with Matt's father as he underwent surgery for prostate cancer. Matt walked through the door of the Kenseth home with a NASCAR Winston Cup Series hat with the race date embroidered on the back and the Subway 400 trophy for his dad. The best post-race interview was done that evening on the couch between father and son.

The following week, Matt was the center of a media blitz in Las Vegas. He had qualified for the Winston No Bull Million last season in Talladega, and DEWALT prepared to launch a $1,000,000 promotion. A wild spin through the infield grass and a loose-handling car produced a 17th-place finish. A few weeks later, Matt went from worst to first at Texas. The DEWALT team fought mechanical issues with their engine and the penalty for changing equaled a 43rd-place starting position. He had finished eighth or better in the last four races. The following week produced a second-place finish at Martinsville. Matt overcame adversity when he raced back onto the lead lap at Richmond and finished sixth, as well as when a cut tire and a

“ I do stand–up once in a while and enjoy making people laugh. As any comic will tell you, we have a pretty high level of expectation when it comes to other people being funny. Matt has kept me laughing for three years. ”

—*Mike Calinoff, Matt's spotter*

ABOVE AND BEYOND

well-timed caution brought him to a second-place showing at Charlotte.

The team had pulled together. Quick pit work earned Matt his first NASCAR Winston Cup pole position and $50,000 with a 13.23 second pit stop at The Winston. Midway through the season, Matt was a steady second in points. Matt's crew was again credited with top-notch pit work when a last-minute gas-and-go put Matt in the lead in Michigan with nine laps remaining. NASCAR threw the red flag with five to go, but Matt opted not to pit and held off challenger Dale Jarrett for win number three.

When Richmond rolled around again in September, Matt was again plagued by tire troubles. Despite going a lap down each time he got a flat tire, the cautions fell in his favor, and he was twice able to race back onto the lead lap. It was a stunning victory. Matt managed to encompass both ends of the spectrum with 16 top-ten finishes, but also nine finishes of 30th or worse. He remained the winningest driver, but was too inconsistent to tame the points system.

When Matt did experience trouble, he was running up front. At Sears Point, the car suffered a broken gear while running third and at Pocono a second-place run was thwarted by a broken transmission. During the fall race at Charlotte, Matt was in contention for the win when he experienced his first engine failure of the year. At Rockingham, the DEWALT Pit Crew for the second time won the Pit Crew Championship.

As his banner season was coming to a close, Matt secured his fifth win of the season at Phoenix International Raceway. It was an emotional victory for Matt who had become a frequent visitor of Victory Lane. The last race of the year was at Homestead. Tony Stewart and Mark Martin were cemented in the top two positions, but less than 100 points separated positions three through eight. A good run for Matt could bump him up to as high as fourth, but due to an engine failure, Matt finished eighth in the final point standings with five wins, 11 top fives and 19 top tens.

CHAPTER 19

DOUBLE DUTY

Although Matt's focus would clearly remain on NASCAR Winston Cup, a tinge of loyalty brought him back to compete in the NASCAR Busch Series in 2003. Reiser Enterprises, comprised of John and Alice Reiser, their son Robbie, and two daughters, had given Matt the opportunity that he needed to break into the ranks of NASCAR. Plagued in 2002 with poor sponsorship backing, Reiser Enterprises had

> **" I know we have a great team. It's been amazing to be able to win all these races this year. It's been unbelievable. "**
>
> *—Matt Kenseth on his winning five races in 2002*

(photo by Doug Hornickel)

struggled and then accepted their inability to run competitively. When John put together a deal with the Bayer Corporation for 20 races, Matt agreed to drive.

The NASCAR Busch Series has previously been the launching pad for recent NASCAR Winston Cup regulars Jeff Green, Kevin Harvick, Steve Park, Jimmie Johnson, Casey Mears and Jamie McMurray. In '98 and '99, Matt and Dale Jr. regularly raced against Joe Nemechek, Terry Labonte, Jeff Burton and Mark Martin. For them, it was valuable practice against their future competition. When Matt raced a limited schedule in the NASCAR Busch Series and the full schedule in the NASCAR Winston Cup Series in 2000 and 2001, it gave him coveted seat time and experience to use on Sundays.

Pulling double duty is time consuming, but Matt, with his competitive spirit, always wanted to race whenever it was possible. The NASCAR Winston Cup crew put in overtime as well, pitting the NASCAR Busch Series car on Saturday, and

ABOVE AND BEYOND

Katie, her sister Julie and mom Karen are big fans of Matt.
(photo by Doug Hornickel)

then running back to the NASCAR Winston Cup garage for adjustments during Happy Hour. Whether it was the Lycos Chevy in '98, the DEWALT Chevy in '99, the Visine Chevy in 2000 and 2001, or the Bayer Ford in 2003, Matt's NASCAR Busch Series rides have all spent time in victory lane. Matt is tenth on the all-time list of NASCAR Busch Series wins with successes at Daytona, Rockingham, California, Dover, Bristol, Charlotte and Pikes Peak.

The 2003 opener at Daytona was like a flashback, watching Dale Jr. and Matt competing and finishing one-two respectively. Although promising NASCAR Busch Series runs were thwarted at Vegas and Texas, Matt experienced back-to-back victories at California Speedway and Lowe's Motor Speedway a few weeks later. Matt's self-control and maturity were

evident at Dover, when after dominating the majority of the race, he spun the tires on the restart and sustained some damage to his car—then later spun trying to hold off Joe Nemechek for the win. Never complaining, he accepted that he made a mistake. He tried too hard. He settled for sixth.

Plan on Matt continuing to race in the NASCAR Busch Series for years to come. With Reiser's team and Kenseth's talent—plan on Matt continuing to win too.

ABOVE AND BEYOND

CHAPTER 20

CATCH ME if YOU CAN

Early into 2003, Jack Roush put rumors of Matt Kenseth moving to another team to rest by re-signing him—along with his teammate, Robbie Reiser—through the 2006 season. Smirnoff Ice Triple Black shared sponsorship with DEWALT with a "Be Smart, Drink Responsibly" campaign for eight races and DEWALT Tools renewed its commitment to Roush Racing and Matt through the 2006 season as well. Although two key players from the DEWALT pit crew departed to pursue other opportunities, a majority of the championship crew remained poised and ready to delve into a promising new season. Heading into the Daytona 500, Matt's previous performances on the temperamental track were an issue. The past year's restrictor plate races had been their fall cards and the unknown loomed ever present. Despite all of their preparation, the team could only hope for the

(photo by Doug Hornickel)

best. Early in the week Matt finished third in his first ever Budweiser Shootout. DeWALT was again launching its Million Dollar Challenge and the flamed Ford fared well through the race. Matt was disappointed with his performance in the Gatorade 125s relinquishing him to a 36th starting place for

Sunday's race. Rain brought out the red flag for the second and final time on lap 129 and Matt recorded a 20th-place finish. After finishing second in Saturday's NASCAR Busch Series race, Matt felt he could have gotten more out of his NASCAR Winston Cup car but for the first time in a while managed to avoid getting caught up in "the big one."

Rockingham followed and Matt posted a third-place finish after running competitively all day, which shot him up to sixth in the NASCAR Winston Cup points standings. Although the NASCAR Busch Series race at Las Vegas was a bitter disappointment with continual mechanical problems, Matt began Sunday in 17th place and worked his way methodically to the front. Once he hit clean air, he dominated the remainder of the race and found his way to Victory Lane. The tried and true teamwork of pit crew, crew chief, spotter and driver that the DeWALT team had been receiving acclaim for pulled it together for Matt's seventh career win and the 269th win for Roush Racing. Heading into Atlanta, Matt jumped from sixth to second in the point standings, a mere three points out of first. It was hard to believe that Matt struggled with a power steering failure at Atlanta. He charged from a 23rd-place starting position and remained firmly planted in the top ten throughout the day. His car was especially good on the "long runs," a trademark of the DeWALT teams car setups. This

> **"That's the thing about Matt. He can take a 40th-place car and finish 20th with it...Matt never quits..."**
>
> *—Roy Kenseth*

top-five finish rewarded him with a 49-point lead in the NASCAR Winston Cup standings—his first ever visit to the top.

As the series progressed to Darlington, a track known as "The Track Too Tough to Tame," Matt said, "I love Darlington. It's a great track, but you either love it or hate it." Robbie prepared for Darlington no differently than he does for any other track. They took the car they ran at Rockingham. Strategy included keeping an eye on the handling of the car and good, fast work in the pits. After an early spin, Matt sustained severe damage, forcing him to pit without the leaders. Matt showed his resilient, unshakable style and never-quit attitude the rest of the day as he refused to be beaten by circumstances. The team continued to make adjustments based on tire wear, handling and changes in track climate to run as high as third, and finally finished eighth.

Next it was time to check Matt's reaction time at Bristol. Teammate Kurt Busch snagged his second victory of the year although the No. 17 Roush Ford of Matt's was a threat for the win as well—Matt settled for second. With a season beginning with five top-ten finishes, the points lead and a flashy new paint scheme, Matt was anxious to head back to Texas as the defending race winner. He led laps, avoided accidents and made the best of ill-timed cautions and pit stops to garnish a sixth-place finish.

The quiet driver was making his presence known. Week after week Matt worked his way through the field, leading laps, making the right adjustments and driving like a seasoned pro. Track announcers began to compare Matt to David Pearson and Alan Kulwicki. In fact, they were even picking him to win races. He was gaining a reputation as one who shunned the spotlight, when in reality, it had never been offered before. Even after winning five races in 2002, his eighth-place points finish didn't garner him predictions of being a championship contender next year. Matt was becoming comfortable with the media blitz, but his focus stayed intent on the race ahead.

Smirnoff Ice-sponsored late model at Madison International Speedway on May 9, 2003. *(photo by Doug Hornickel)*

After yet another top-ten finish at Talladega, the competitor in Matt seemed slightly miffed at the unpredictable friendships made during closing laps in superspeedway races. It's every man for himself, but you can't win the restrictor plate races without pushes.

Matt's worst finish of the season to date came at Martinsville—the only track where he did not complete every lap. Uncomfortable in his car, Matt radioed in unsavory descriptions of the DeWALT Ford "plowing through the center," and "so loose it was like driving on ice." Running as low as 40th, he came home 22nd. Matt's dad Roy accepted his son's rough run saying, "That's the thing about Matt. He can take a 40th-place car and finish 20th with it. A lot of other drivers might give up, but Matt never quits working on his car and trying to get more out of it than seems possible." Even after a disappointing day, Matt didn't complain to the press. "We just ran real badly. Everybody worked on it hard and we got it respectable at the end if we could do a real, real long run, but it just won't go

"We're still having a career-best year for this team, and Matt (Kenseth, point leader) is having some kind of an all-time best-ever season. We're going to keep doing what we have been doing."

—Dale Jr.

anywhere. That's all we had."

California and Richmond added two more top-ten finishes to Matt's running tally, and he gained respect for his unfailing consistency early on in 2003.

Like many other drivers residing in North Carolina, heading to Lowe's for The Winston and the Coca-Cola 600 is like going home for a while. Matt headed back to his other home in Wisconsin to help his father promote their local track with a DeWALT-sponsored night of racing. More than 11,000 fans packed the track past capacity to see Matt dominate his old stomping grounds and tear up the track with a late model. The support from the Midwestern crowd was overwhelming. There was literally a sea of yellow and black, fans showing their colors, paying homage to their local hero. When Matt arrived back to his southern home, he was pumped to shine under the lights at The Winston. With a sixth-place finish in the all-star event, Matt had every intention of racing to win on the following Sunday evening. Rain soaked nearly every event of the 2003 season, and whether it was showers or torrents, it meant the same thing—a wet track. In 2002, Matt diced through traffic chasing Mark Martin to finish second. Now in 2003, Matt was running in second again when the 600 was red flagged for a second time for rain, and eventually halted—crowning Jimmie Johnson the winner. Instead of being satisfied with a bigger spread in the points, the racer in Matt was more than disappointed. "I'd be happy right now if we could race 130 more laps and I'd finish fourth than to finish second and call it off early."

Dover, Kenseth's favorite track, was next on the list. Matt rolled off in his best starting position of the year-fourth. All day the team fought with a loose car and never got the adjustments quite right. Matt finished seventh. Matt's record at Pocono was a consistent finish in the top 15 in the last six starts. During the race, they cut it short on fuel and ran out as they were coming in for a pit stop. The engine stalled, making the stop a costly one, but they remained on the lead lap. Matt finished a career-best third at Pocono. Returning to Michigan, the site of last year's spring victory, was a welcome sight. Roy was with his son on Father's Day. They had a good car. One stop yielded a bad set of tires, but they ran up front most of the day. With five laps to go, Matt gave up track position for a four-tire stop and restarted ninth. In the last five laps, Matt improved five positions to finish fourth. The next two races on the schedule were critical for the points battle. Matt's record at both Sonoma (three finishes of 21, 32, and 39) and Daytona (only one top ten in seven starts) threatened his points lead. It was an up-and-down day. They ran in the top five and then in the mid-20s. But Sonoma rewarded Matt with a 14th-place finish, his best to date. The DEWALT crew attributed their improvement to a testing session two months prior. Daytona, under the lights in July, showcased the Smirnoff Ice Triple Black car. Early on, Matt overshot his pit box, but

teamwork prevailed and it made no lasting impact on their run. On the last handful of laps, Matt drafted with teammate Greg Biffle. Robbie radioed to Matt that they would be three laps short on fuel. Matt replied, "Are you sure we can't make it?" Robbie was firm in his judgment, and they elected to pit with less than 20 laps to go. Matt finished sixth, his best ever Daytona finish, and teammate Biffle picked up his first win. At the midway point in the season, the DEWALT team brought chassis MMR19 to Chicago, the same car that finished second at Lowe's in May. Matt finished 12th after struggling with the handling on the car. "It was a terrible day with a decent finish," Matt said. Despite his disappointment, Matt came through the first half of the year with one win, seven top fives and 14 top tens. He was 165 points ahead of second-place Jeff Gordon, and nearly 400 points ahead of fifth place.

> ## "Are you sure we can't make it?"
> —*Matt Kenseth*

(photo by Doug Hornickel)

ABOVE AND BEYOND

CHAPTER 21

MR. CONSISTENCY

One of the benefits of being the points leader is starting on the pole when qualifying washes out. Matt led the field on lap one at Loudon and collected five bonus points. On lap two, he took it a little hot into the turn and slipped to sixth. On lap 143, Matt overshot his pit, a rare mistake for the season's smoothest operator. Restarting 16th, it was an up-and-down day filled with cautions and fuel mileage scenarios. Matt managed to avoid

trouble, conserve fuel and finished third. The following week, Matt ran in the top five all day at Pocono. Again fuel mileage played a part and the DEWALT team opted to pit, just to be sure. When it was over, Matt finished 13th, wondering whether or not he had given away any points. "We had a second- or third-place car and finished 13th with it. You just can't do that. You give away too many points. When you play conservative, that's when

(photo by James Rapp)

could have caused the temperature of the engine to rise to a dangerous level. Yet after a few laps, the degrees dropped and the only heat generated was through Matt's blistering laps on the track. Midway through the race, he charged from 12th to fifth. The checkered flag waved for Kevin Harvick, Kenseth was just a few laps short of taking the win himself.

Watkins Glen and Michigan netted Kenseth another pair of top tens to add to his collection. Most fans think the traffic is bad just trying to get into Bristol, the drivers think it's pretty thick on the track. Matt's fourth-place finish garnered him a 351-point advantage over Dale Jr. heading into Darlington. The last Southern 500 was memorable for Matt. It was one of the few times he finished outside of the top ten in 2003. Kenseth was strong early on, leading laps. After a caution, teammate Jeff Burton beat Matt out of the pits, and a duel for the lead yielded the Smirnoff Ice Triple Black Ford a Darlington Stripe. No one could accuse Matt of "points racing" after his stout run. Matt struggled the remainder of the day—the car was

you get bit. They said that's all the fuel we had, but I don't know, everybody else made it." Matt set his disappointments aside the following week at Indy, where he started 17th. Escaping disaster was the name of the game. A run-in with Bobby Labonte damaged the grille of the #17 car and

too loose, not turning out the needed power, or simply not adjusted correctly. After the race Matt admitted, "I was trying to lead the most laps, and it was dumb. I should have let Burton go and race the race track like you're supposed to do here and wait until the end. It could have been worse, but we had a shot to win so it kind of hurts." Still Matt gained another 38 points in his quest for the NASCAR Winston Cup. Three straight top-ten finishes at Richmond, Loudon and Dover and Matt led the series by an astounding 436 points.

Talladega would be the first of two setbacks. The first engine failure of the year relegated the DEWALT team to a 37th-place finish. Their hopes of bouncing back at Kansas, instead were dashed when they mirrored their worst finish of the year —37th again. Still a whopping 259 points up on second-place Kevin Harvick, the media was getting a glimmer of hope for some sort of a points race. Charlotte was nothing short of a wrestling match between Harvick and Kenseth, the Goodwrench

Matt is pushed to the pits at Kansas Speedway after a near collision with Michael Waltrip on lap 69.
(photo by David Bogard)

Chevy and special paint scheme Carhartt Ford pushed and shoved for position on the track. Matt went on to pass Harvick and slide by Dale Jr. for a triumphant eighth-place finish. Matt finished barely outside the top ten with a 13th at Martinsville and an 11th at Atlanta the following weeks. Returning to Phoenix, the site of last year's fifth win, Matt was again back on track and running

> **"When you get a guy like Matt who has been on a roll all year, you can't fault the system. He's having a good year. Let him enjoy it and reap the rewards from it. He deserves it. There shouldn't be a change in the points system to take that away from him."**
>
> —*Tony Stewart on Matt Kenseth's running away with the championship in 2003*

away with the championship. Matt started 37th and was impressed with his team's effort. Pit stops were less than 13 seconds, and Matt continued to pick up places on the track. Unable to motor past Michael Waltrip in the closing laps, Matt settled for sixth place. With two races remaining, Matt only needed to finish 30th or better to take home the NASCAR Winston Cup trophy; regardless of what any other competitor was able to accomplish.

(photo by James Rapp)

ABOVE AND BEYOND

COMING FULL CIRCLE

Matt needed to leave the North Carolina Speedway with a 186-point lead to clinch the NASCAR Winston Cup Championship. The number ended up being 226. Plenty of attention was directed at Kenseth and the DEWALT team when the green flag waved that Sunday. Matt began in the middle of the pack, dropping back to 30th on the first run. Hearts dropped when Matt checked up to avoid a crash

Matt's mom Nicki celebrates as Matt locks up the NASCAR Winston Cup championship. *(photo by Doug Hornickel)*

(photo by Doug Hornickel)

and Tony Stewart made contact. He controlled the swerve and plodded on. Stewart's team was quick to apologize for getting into him. Midway into the race, during a long green run, Matt cracked the top ten. The points "as they run" showed Matt on his way to the title. As Matt headed into the pits on lap 242, the caution waved. Even though he was past the commitment line, Kenseth dodged back out onto the track, and readily accepted the penalty—tail end of the longest line. Sixth place. His closest point challenger, Dale Earnhardt, Jr., was caught a lap down in the mid-teens. Matt never fell back farther than fifth the last 100 laps. It was a glorious run with the checkered flag flying as Matt crossed the line in fourth place. Matt Kenseth is the last NASCAR Winston Cup Champion. Two

Winston trucks picked up the crew on pit road and followed the DeWALT Ford around the "Rock" for a victory lap. Matt revved up the engine and did some donuts in the grass before exiting his car. An emotional Kenseth said, "It's unbelievable. This is beyond my wildest dreams. I never thought I'd ever have the opportunity to sit in one of these cars, much less be the champion." Matt was joined in Victory Lane by his proud father Roy. He held back no emotion, hugging his son and saying, "I'm so proud of you."

Matt's championship would be the first NASCAR Winston Cup championship for Jack Roush (Jack has several championships within other NASCAR series). Teammates Jeff Burton and Mark Martin were among the first to stop by to congratulate Matt. Mark Martin said, "I've been wrong about a lot of things in my life, but I was right about Matt Kenseth. I'm real proud of that."

Back home, where it all began in the little town of Cambridge, hundreds of local folks were celebrating in their own way. A large gathering of friends and family had waited anxiously at a sports bar, wanting to share the moment of victory together. The local Fire Department immediately erected a sign on top of their firehouse and drove through town with their sirens flashing and Kenseth hats waving out the fire truck windows. Even though one race remained in the 2003 season, for Cambridge residents, it was over.

It was a glorious run with the checkered flag flying as Matt crossed the line in fourth place. Matt Kenseth is the last NASCAR Winston Cup Champion.

(photos by Doug Hornickel)

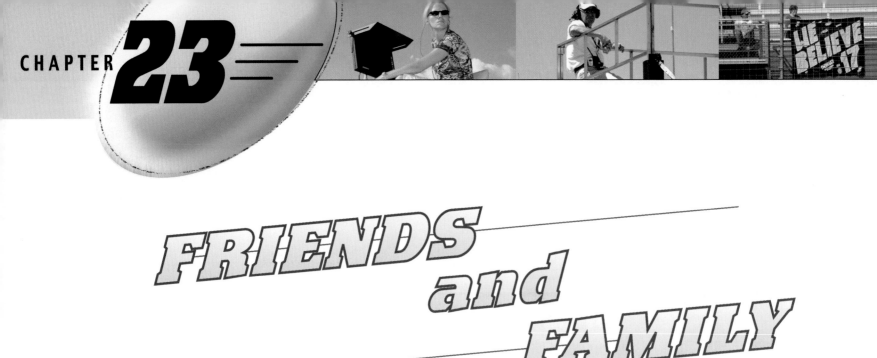

CHAPTER 23

FRIENDS and FAMILY

When Matt met his wife Katie, his biggest fan was born. Supportive and sweet, Katie took a serious interest in her husband's career.

Matt is a cool, clean competitor who loves to race. But he's also a husband, father, brother and son. With a father who shared his son's passion for racing, the two spent much time traveling in the early years while Matt was getting his career underway. When Matt made the transition into the NASCAR Busch Series, Matt's dad Roy traveled with his son to many races. When Matt won his first NASCAR Busch Series race in

1998, father and son were charged with emotion and gratitude.

When Matt met his wife Katie, his biggest fan was born. Supportive and sweet, Katie took a serious interest in her husband's career. Trading in a college degree for a life of travel, she gladly began to live and learn the ropes of professional racing. Katie is Matt's silent crew chief. She watches every lap on top of the pit box— calculating, hoping and praying. When Matt's in the garage for practice, Katie's watching from on top of their motor coach. When it's time to qualify, she walks down with the DEWALT car space by space, chatting with friends and the crew, just spending time with her husband. Race days she is always by his side. After introductions, she watches him strap into the car, shares a prayer with the chaplain and Matt, and gives him a kiss. After

Wisconsin friends and family at the Milwaukee Mile.
(photo by Kelley Maruszewski)

Katie watches, waits and worries. *(photo by Doug Hornickel)*

the race, they head to the airport to fly home. Sometimes they celebrate together in Victory Lane, and sometimes Katie gives Matt some quiet time after a rough race. But they are inseparable and quite content to be so.

Matt's son Ross turned ten in May of 2003 and has begun quite a racing career of his own. He lives in Wisconsin with his mother, Lisa, and her husband, Scott, but when he's not in school he travels frequently to watch his dad run around the big tracks. With NASCAR age restrictions on pit road, Ross might spend a NASCAR Winston Cup

"What's-his-name is so good to me."

—a T-shirt that Katie Kenseth wore in response to the media's constant portrayal of Matt as being "too vanilla."

MATT KENSETH

Sunday at MRO, NASCAR's traveling ministry. One of Motor Racing Outreach's missions is to provide care for drivers' and crews' children so that the wives can be with their husbands on pit road. Motor Racing Outreach has been an influential organization in the lives of Matt and Katie. After they were engaged, they chose Ron Pegram, one of the chaplains at MRO, to perform their wedding ceremony. Katie is active in the Bible studies for women and both Matt and Katie attend Chapel services on Sunday mornings before the races. Matt and Katie have forged a friendship with Dale Beaver, the NASCAR Winston Cup chaplain. He makes a stop by the DEWALT car before every race to join them in prayer.

Roy is as serious about Matt's racing as Matt is. *(photo by Doug Hornickel)*

Katie's parents, Gordy and Karen Martin, frequently travel from Cambridge to spend time with their daughter and son-in-law trackside. Gordy was put to work at Pocono a few years ago, running gas when their regular crewman was unavailable. Their families weave a net of support, whether it's Matt's grandpa Kenseth, who watches every race from his recliner on Sunday, Karen praying for Matt's safety every Sunday morning at church, Matt's dad Roy standing on top of the hauler for hours of practice clocking speeds, or friends from high school who come down to hang out in the pits and get a different view of racing that TV simply can't provide. Matt has a real group of fans and most importantly supporters.

Matt and Katie live in their motor coach in the infield of a track for four days almost every weekend. Within that "high-class trailer park" they've made friends as well. They do the same things every weekend that other families do—barbeque, watch TV, toss around a football, play video games, walk their dogs, and sometimes they cruise around on their golf carts too. Their closest "neighbors" are Jeff and Michelle Green who are frequently parked next to them in the lot. Katie spends a lot of time with her girlfriends Nicole (Greg Biffle's longtime girlfriend) and Krissie (Ryan Newman's fiancée). Matt tends to take care of business first, usually spending time talking to Robbie on the phone about the car, or hooking up with Mark Martin or Jeff Burton to compare notes. At first thought, it may be hard to imagine "NASCAR superstars" hanging out in their sweats, washing their dishes or taking out the garbage, but in reality they aren't any different from anyone else.

Matt and Katie are involved in charity work, mainly with Kyle and Pattie Petty and the Victory Junction Gang. They completed their second Charity Ride this year and frequently contribute to MRO and other charities. Matt visited the Walter Reed Army Hospital in Washington, D.C. on April 28 to visit with soldiers who were injured in Operation Iraqi Freedom and in Afghanistan.

When Matt is not at the track, he can be found at the shop. If he's not at the shop, he can be found at home. Transplanted to North Carolina, Wisconsin natives Matt and Katie had no trouble getting used to the significantly warmer weather. Although snowmobiling is out of the question, they enjoy boating, jet skiing, swimming, gardening and landscaping, decorating their house, and hanging out with Katie's sister Julie, her husband Justin and their baby Sam. But the first order of business upon arriving back home is not laundry or bill paying— it's Lars. Lars is a cat, but he is king of the Kenseth house. Lars may actually hold the world record for ownership of the most toy mice. He's shamelessly loved by Matt and Katie, despite his prerogative to hold a grudge when they are gone too long. Lars used to travel to the racetrack weekly, but after he developed a nasty habit of trashing their motor home when they were gone, he relocated back to Mooresville. When they make the trek back to Wisconsin, they spend time working outside—mowing the yard, chopping up firewood, hunting and fishing and, of course, spending time with their families.

Matt's fans show their support at Atlanta Motor Speedway in 2003.
(photo by Action Sports Photography Inc./ Michael Romano)

CHAPTER 24

THE LAST WORD

(Photo by Kelley Maruszewski)

On Tuesday mornings, Matt grabs a cup of coffee on the way to the shop. He then meets with Robbie, the car chief, the engineer and the shock specialist to talk about the upcoming week. Together they make decisions about which car they want to take and what setup they want to take to the next track. Matt makes sure that he is very involved with the activity at the shop. He stops in a couple of times a week and watches what's

MATT KENSETH

" Matt's driving style is not like a Stewart or a (Kurt) Busch or somebody like that. He's more like a Darrell Waltrip or a Bill Elliott, just smooth. But if you ever watch Matt, Matt can drive the wheels off a race car. ... Matt's probably a little more of an aggressive driver than he's given credit for. I've seen Matt do some things sometimes (and you think), 'Wow, that guy is a heck of a race car driver.' **"**

—*Ray Evernham*

Matt's goals haven't changed since his teenage days of racing. He's out there to run competitively and win races. He's doing both.

going on. "Robbie has such a good handle on it. The better we run, the less time I have to spend at the shop with the guys," Matt says.

Matt spent many more hours at the NASCAR Busch Series shop in the earlier years. "I didn't have any friends, so I hung out at the shop all day. Robbie was trying to organize everything, build the cars and work on the shocks. I tried to learn how they worked. I enjoyed doing it and it passed the time."

Today, Matt's schedule is full. His senior year in NASCAR Winston Cup netted him the NASCAR Winston Cup Championship with one race left in the season. Matt's goals haven't changed since his teenage days of racing. He's out there to run competitively and win races. He's doing both.

What does the future hold for Matt Kenseth? He's seated firmly in the Roush Racing DEWALT Ford. His team improves every year. His experience level only adds to his natural talent. The future can be uncertain, but for Matt, he will continue to go above and beyond.

(photo by Doug Hornickel)

MATT KENSETH
FAST FACTS

Birthdate:
March 10, 1972

Birthplace:
Madison, Wisconsin

Residence:
Mooresville, North Carolina

Family:
wife Katie, son Ross, cat Lars

Favorite Racetrack:
Dover Downs

Hobbies and Interests:
snowmobiling, video games,
motorcycling, boating

Favorite Band:
Metallica

Favorite Sports Team:
Green Bay Packers

Personal Vehicle:
2002 Roush Stage 3 Mustang

COOL THINGS to KNOW

- Matt's Winston Cup Chassis number MMR23 won at Richmond last fall and ran there this spring. MMR stands for Mark Martin Racing. They have cars numbering up to 33. The lowest number is 13, a road course car. The rest have been retired.

- Matt's favorite driver as a kid was Dale Earnhardt. His dad rooted for Mark Martin and Bill Elliott.

- Matt's first car was a 1982 Honda Accord that previously belonged to his older sister. After she managed to smash into enough trees to wreck the front end, it became a lawn ornament behind the Kenseth race shop. Matt worked on it for a month before he could get it running again. His next car was a 1983 Plymouth he bought for $700. He put 25,000 miles on it.

- Matt's best friend is not Mark Martin or Dale Jr. Although Matt spends time with Mark and Jr. at the track, the title goes to Matt Fischer. They've been friends since grade school. They own land near each other in southern Wisconsin and like to hunt and fish, ride four wheelers and start big bonfires. They recently attended the Metallica concert in Boston and met their favorite band.

- Matt made a DeWALT appearance in Appleton, Wisconsin. He landed his jet in a Wisconsin airport and picked up his grandpa, Helmer Kenseth. Ninety-four-year-old Helmer flew co-pilot from there to Appleton.

MATT KENSETH TIMELINE

1972

- Matthew Roy Kenseth is born to Roy and Nicki Kenseth

1988

- Begins racing career at age 16 at Columbus 151 Speedway
- Wins late model feature in his third start

1988-91

- Scores 14 late model main event wins
- Earns the nickname "Matt the Brat" from media for consistently beating the more established veteran racers

1991

- Wins late model Rookie of the Year award at Wisconsin International Raceway, Kaukauna, Wisconsin
- Youngest driver (at 19) ever to win an ARTGO racing series feature event, winning at LaCrosse Fairgrounds Speedway; Mark Martin previously held the record

1993

- Wins late model Rookie of the Year award at Slinger Speedway

• Totals 13 main event wins in 1993 including the Alan Kulwicki Memorial at Slinger Speedway; the ARTGO 100 at Norway (Michigan) Speedway; the Wisconsin Short Track Series 200 at Madison International Speedway; and the Oktoberfest 100 at LaCrosse Fairgrounds Speedway

1994

• Wins 18 late model feature events
• Wins track championships at Wisconsin International Raceway and Madison International Speedway
• Completes 100 percent of the laps at both tracks
• Captures first Miller Genuine Draft Nationals title (Slinger and Madison)

1996

• NASCAR Busch Series debut in No. 55 Chevy rented from Bobby Dotter
• Timed in 29th out of 70 cars; finishes fifth in the 40-lap last chance race; in the Red Dog 300, Matt stays out of trouble and finishes 31st

1997

• Joins Reiser Enterprises's NASCAR Busch Series team in April and finishes sixth in Nashville debut

1998

- Wins first NASCAR Busch Series Race on February 21 at Rockingham, with a late race nudge to Tony Stewart
- Earns first pole position at Pikes Peak
- Wins two more races at Pikes Peak and Dover Downs
- Starts first NASCAR Winston Cup race subbing for Bill Elliott; finishes sixth
- Finishes second in the NASCAR Busch Series standings to Dale Earnhardt Jr.

1999

- Breaks track qualifying record at Dover Downs
- Wins four NASCAR Busch Series races and leads point standings early in the year
- Finishes third in the NASCAR Busch Series standings to Dale Earnhardt Jr. and Jeff Green
- Makes five NASCAR Winston Cup starts with top finish of fourth at Dover

2000

- Wins NASCAR Busch Series opener at Daytona
- Wins four more NASCAR Busch Series races at California, Dover and Charlotte bringing his career total to 11 victories
- First rookie ever to win the Coca-Cola 600 at Charlotte
- Wins Raybestos Rookie of the Year, triumphing over six other drivers
- Finishes 13th in NASCAR Winston Cup point standings

2001

- Finishes 12th in NASCAR Winston Cup point standings
- DeWALT crew wins World Championship Pit Crew Competition

2002

- Wins the series high total of five NASCAR Winston Cup races at Rockingham, Texas, Michigan, Richmond and Phoenix
- Quick pit work and blistering driving earns the DeWALT team the pole position for The Winston at Lowe's Motor Speedway
- Captures his first NASCAR Winston Cup pole at Dover Downs
- DeWALT crew wins second consecutive World Championship Pit Crew Competition
- Finishes eighth in final NASCAR Winston Cup point standings

2003

- Re-signs with Roush Racing
- Scores seventh NASCAR Winston Cup victory at Las Vegas
- NASCAR Busch Series wins at Charlotte and California
- Takes NASCAR Winston Cup points lead at Atlanta in March
- Wins NASCAR Winston Cup Championship

MATT KENSETH FAN CLUB

Matt's Fan Club was formed by his father, Roy Kenseth, in 1997. Matt's grandpa was the first member, and Gloria Melton of the small hometown newspaper, *The Cambridge News*, was second. Based in Matt's hometown of Cambridge, Wisconsin, the fan club expanded from the Kenseth living room to a storefront with memorabilia, merchandise and one of Matt's early NASCAR Busch Series racecars.

2004 Fan Club members receive an autographed 8 x 10 hero card, membership card, stickers, and quarterly newsletters. If you would like to join the Matt Kenseth Fan Club, please send $20 ($15 + $5 S&H) to: MKFC, 10 Water Street, Cambridge, WI, 53523 or you can join online at *www.mattkenseth.com.*

2003 RACE STATS

2003 Totals

Starts	Avg. Start	Provisionals Used	Avg. Finish	Points	% Laps Complete	Winnings
36	21.3	7	10.2	5022	97.0%	$4,038,120

Race	Start	Finish	Points	Standing Position	Laps/Total	Winnings	Status
Daytona 500	35	20	108	19	109/109	$200,345	Running
Subway 400	18	3	170	6	393/393	$94,350	Running
UAW-DaimlerChrysler 400	17	1	180	2	267/267	$365,875	Running
Bass Pro Shops MBNA 500	24	4	160	1	325/325	$91,850	Running
Carolina Dodge Dealers 400	12	8	142	1	293/293	$69,440	Running
Food City 500	37	2	175	1	500/500	$118,870	Running
Samsung/RadioShack 500	17	6	155	1	334/334	$142,950	Running
Aaron's 499	27	9	143	1	188/188	$104,730	Running
Virginia 500	34	22	97	1	499/500	$66,725	Running
Auto Club 500	23	9	143	1	250/250	$95,425	Running
Pontiac Excitement 400	18	7	146	1	393/393	$73,675	Running
Coca-Cola 600	18	2	180	1	276/27	$206,500	Running
MBNA Armed Forces Family 400	4	7	146	1	400/400	$87,985	Running
Pocono 500	25	3	170	1	200/200	$109,870	Running
Sirius 400	21	4	160	1	200/200	$93,275	Running
Dodge/Save Mart 350	4	14	121	1	110/110	$78,975	Running
Pepsi 400	37	6	155	1	160/160	$98,475	Running
Tropicana 400	24	12	127	1	266/267	$87,725	Running
New England 300	1	3	170	1	300/300	$124,030	Running
Pennsylvania 500	9	13	129	1	200/200	$68,590	Running
Brickyard 400	17	2	175	1	160/160	$314,425	Running
Sirius at the Glen	7	8	142	1	90/90	$70,535	Running
GFS Marketplace 400	33	9	138	1	200/200	$76,540	Running
Sharpie 500	10	4	160	1	500/500	$122,905	Running
Mountain Dew Southern 500	6	14	126	1	367/367	$75,720	Running
Chevy Rock & Roll 400	18	7	146	1	400/400	$75,230	Running
Sylvania 300	19	7	151	1	300/300	$80,750	Running
MBNA America 400	1	9	143	1	400/400	$79,840	Running
EA SPORTS 500	37	33	69	1	158/188	$61,125	Engine
Banquet 400 presented by ConAgra Foods	37	36	55	1	220/267	$68,575	Running
UAW-GM Quality 500	29	8	142	1	334/334	$82,425	Running
Subway 500	14	13	124	1	500/500	$68,400	Running
Bass Pro Shops MBNA 500	37	11	130	1	325/325	$95,825	Running
Checker Auto Parts 500 presented by Havoline	37	6	150	1	312/312	$86,000	Running
Pop Secret Microwave Popcorn 400	23	4	160	1	393/393	$92,650	Running
Ford 400	37	43	34	1	28/267	$62,665	Engine

Celebrate the Heroes of Auto Racing
in These Other Releases from Sports Publishing!

Jack Arute's Tales from the Indy 500
by Jack Arute and Jenna Fryer

- 5.5 x 8.25 hardcover
- 200 pages
- photos throughout
- $19.95
- 2004 release!

The Sands of Time: Celebrating 100 Years of Racing at Daytona
by Bill Lazarus

- 10 x 10 hardcover
- 192 pages
- photos throughout
- $29.95
- Includes a companion DVD!
- 2004 release!

Mark Martin: Mark of Excellence
by Larry Woody

- 10 x 10 hardcover
- 160 pages
- color photos throughout
- $24.95
- 2004 release!

Mark Martin: Ozark Original
by Kathy Persinger

- 5.5 x 7 softcover
- 96 pages
- photos throughout
- $5.95
- 2004 release!

Ryan Newman: Engineer for Speed
by Deb Williams

- 10 x 10 hardcover
- 210 pages
- photos throughout
- $24.95
- 2004 release!

Ryan Newman: From Purdue to Penske
by Deb Williams

- 5.5 x 7 hardcover
- 96 pages
- photos throughout
- $5.95
- 2004 release!

Kenny Bernstein: King of Speed
by Kenny Bernstein with Bill Stephens

- 10 x 10 hardcover
- 160 pages
- color photos throughout
- $24.95
- 2004 release!

Tales from the Drag Strip with "Big Daddy" Don Garlits
by Don Garlits with Bill Stephens

- 5.5 x 8.25 hardcover
- 200 pages
- photos throughout
- $19.95
- 2004 release!

Bobby Allison: A Racer's Racer
by Bobby Allison with Tim Packman

- 10 x 10 hardcover
- 128 pages
- color photos throughout
- $29.95
- Includes an audio CD!

Tony Stewart: High Octane in the Fast Lane
by The Associated Press and AP/WWP

- 10 x 10 hardcover
- 160 pages
- color photos throughout
- $39.95
- Includes an audio CD!

Lowe's Motor Speedway: A Weekend at the Track
by Kathy Persinger

- 8.5 x 11 hardcover
- 128 pages
- color photos throughout
- $24.95

Atlanta Motor Speedway: A Weekend at the Track
by Kathy Persinger

- 8 1/2 x 11 hardcover
- 128 pages
- color photos throughout
- $24.95

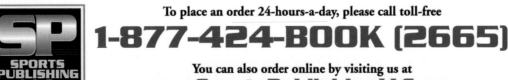